EASY
GUIDE TO
SPANISH

EASY
GUIDE TO
SPANISH

FALL RIVER PRESS

New York

FALL RIVER PRESS

New York

An Imprint of Sterling Publishing
387 Park Avenue South
New York, NY 10016

© 2005, 2004 by Spark Publishing

Cover design by *the*BookDesigners
Written by Rebecca Ortman
©Shutterstock/Ozerina Anna
©Shutterstock/Renzo.luo

ISBN 978-1-4351-4707-2

Distributed in Canada by Sterling Publishing
c/o Canadian Manda Group, 165 Dufferin Street
Toronto, Ontario, Canada M6K 3H6
Distributed in the United Kingdom by GMC Distribution Services
Castle Place, 166 High Street, Lewes, East Sussex, England BN7 1XU
Distributed in Australia by Capricorn Link (Australia) Pty. Ltd.
P.O. Box 704, Windsor, NSW 2756, Australia

For information about custom editions, special sales, and premium and
corporate purchases, please contact Sterling Special Sales at
800-805-5489 or specialsales@sterlingpublishing.com.

Manufactured in the United States of America

2   4   6   8   10   9   7   5   3   1

www.sterlingpublishing.com

CONTENTS

INTRODUCTION
TRUE CONFESSIONS

My name is Olivia Lane, and I have a confession to make. I'm completely addicted to *Passions*. I mean, sure, I love *General Hospital, Days of Our Lives,* and *The Bold and the Beautiful*. But *Passions* is my guilty pleasure. Yes, I know it's ranked dead last among soaps, and some of the "actors" really never should have been actors at all, and my friends are always telling me how terrible it is, but COME ON! Lighten up, people. It's *funny*. I think it's a bit of a contradiction when people say they love soaps, yet they take themselves so seriously they can't admit they enjoy the *fun* one. (I know for a fact my friends can't resist sneaking a peek at it now and then, even though they deny it. How else would they be able to make fun of it?)

My name's Olivia, by the way. Aside from watching soap operas, I also happen to be really good at failing Spanish, which I managed to do this past spring. And I'm talking an F, not even a D or something remotely salvageable. Part of the problem was that Spanish was my last class, 2:15–3:00, right before *Passions*. Anyway, my dad and *la profesora* cooked up this little scheme for me: I would go and study Spanish abroad during the summer on the Spanish Club trip to Costa Rica. Then I could come back and take a test, and if I passed Profesora would move me on to Spanish II. That would also mean my big fat F wouldn't show up on my official transcript, which, as Dad points out, would make it a bit hard to get into a good college.

I AM A COMPLETE DORK

I was immediately given membership in the Spanish Club at school, as well as the Instituto Español de Costa Rica group. The "I Am A Complete Dork" buttons were surely on their way, too. We had a few group meetings so everyone on the trip could meet each other. Most of the participants were total Spanish nuts—I mean gung-ho Spanish freaks who knew more than the teacher. There was only one other freshman, and, as my luck would have it, it was Blair Whittermore. Blair Whittermore is one of those overachievers whom no one would want to spend a month alone with in a strange country. Blair's snottiness is practically unrivalled.

But I did find out one thing about Costa Rica that should make the trip quite bearable: the siesta! Do you know what that means? It means that from 1–5 everyone goes home and eats a big meal and takes a nap or watches TV. TV! Soaps! Are you following me? Just when I thought that I'd be deprived of *Passions* for a whole month! I mean, in this age of satellite dishes and digital cable, my host family is bound to get *Passions,* right?

Barnes & Noble Booksellers #2831
4300 Montgomery Road
Ellicott City, MD 21043
410-203-9001

STR:2831 REG:004 TRN:5453 CSHR:William D

Easy Guide to Spanish
  9781435147072   11
  (1 @ 5.98) PROMO 50% (2.99)
  (1 @ 2.99)   2.99

Subtotal   2.99
Sales Tax T1 (6.000%)   0.18
TOTAL   3.17
VISA DEBIT   3.17
  Card#: XXXXXXXXXXXX5435

A MEMBER WOULD HAVE SAVED   0.30

Thanks for shopping at
Barnes & Noble

Like Barnes and Noble Long Gate Shopping Ctr
on Facebook

101.348   07/10/2014 02:50PM

CUSTOMER COPY

and undamaged music CDs, DVDs, and audio books made within 14 days of purchase from a Barnes & Noble Booksellers store or Barnes & Noble.com with the below exceptions:

A store credit for the purchase price will be issued (i) for purchases made by check less than 7 days prior to the date of return, (ii) when a gift receipt is presented within 60 days of purchase, (iii) for textbooks, or (iv) for products purchased at Barnes & Noble College bookstores that are listed for sale in the Barnes & Noble Booksellers inventory management system.

Opened music CDs/DVDs/audio books may not be returned, and can be exchanged only for the same title and only if defective. NOOKs purchased from other retailers or sellers are returnable only to the retailer or seller from which they are purchased, pursuant to such retailer's or seller's return policy. Magazines, newspapers, eBooks, digital downloads, and used books are not returnable or exchangeable. Defective NOOKs may be exchanged at the store in accordance with the applicable warranty.

Returns or exchanges will not be permitted (i) after 14 days or without receipt or (ii) for product not carried by Barnes & Noble or Barnes & Noble.com.

Policy on receipt may appear in two sections.

Return Policy

With a sales receipt or Barnes & Noble.com packing slip, a full refund in the original form of payment will be issued from any Barnes & Noble Booksellers store for returns of undamaged NOOKs, new and unread books, and unopened and undamaged music CDs, DVDs, and audio books made within 14 days of purchase from a Barnes & Noble Booksellers store or Barnes & Noble.com with the below exceptions:

A store credit for the purchase price will be issued (i) for purchases made by check less than 7 days prior to the date of return, (ii) when a gift receipt is presented within 60 days of purchase, (iii) for textbooks, or (iv) for products purchased at Barnes & Noble College

YOU MAY ALSO LIKE...

Easy Guide to Math
   by SparkNotes

Doodle Yourself Smart ... Math
   by Helen Greaves

Drive & Learn Spanish: A Language Course
   by Howard Beckerman

Complete Wilderness Training Manual
   by Hugh McManners

Who's (oops) Whose Grammar Book Is This...
   by C. Edward Good

bookstores that are listed for sale in the Barnes & Noble Booksellers inventory management system.

Opened music CDs/DVDs/audio books may not be returned, and can be exchanged only for the same title and only if defective. NOOKs purchased from other retailers or sellers are returnable only to the retailer or seller from which they are purchased, pursuant to such retailer's or seller's return policy. Magazines, newspapers, eBooks, digital downloads, and used books are not returnable or exchangeable. Defective NOOKs may be exchanged at the store in accordance with the applicable warranty.

Returns or exchanges will not be permitted (i) after 14 days or without receipt or (ii) for product not carried by Barnes & Noble or Barnes & Noble.com.

Policy on receipt may appear in two sections.

Return Policy

With a sales receipt or Barnes & Noble.com packing slip, a full refund in the original form of payment will be issued

EASY GUIDE TO
SPANISH

CHAPTER 1
PRONUNCIATION

I make it through about five pages of *Soap Opera Digest* before falling asleep on the plane. When I wake up, we're touching down in San José, Costa Rica.

Upon arrival we're immediately whisked over to Immigration. Somehow, most of the class gets in one line to get their passports stamped, and I wind up in another. Everyone looks quite serious, which is no wonder since there are drug-sniffing dogs and soldiers with machine guns all over the place. Soon I'm at the front, and I hand my passport to the man. He stares at me and then at the photo like I'm some common criminal. To be helpful I spell out my last name. *L-A-N-E*. However, as I watch him write it, I see that he's spelled *L-E-N-I*.

"Um, excuse me?" I ask.

"*¿Perdóname?*"[1] the man says looking up at me.

"Look," I say, pointing at his form. "You've spelled my name wrong."

"*¿Cómo?*"[2]

"I'm sorry, but it appears you've spelled my name wrong," I say. "*L-A-N-E.* With an *a* and an *e. E-E-E-E-E,*" I say, very clearly.

"*Sí,* Leni *con un* e *o* i."[3]

"No, that's an *i,*" I say. "*Lane* is spelled with an *a* and an *e* at the end." The man stares at me a long while and then motions over a soldier carrying a machine gun roughly the size of a small child. Uh-oh. The two men whisper together and look me up and down for quite some time. Then the director of the trip, Andrés, comes over. He lives in Costa Rica and runs the school where we'll be studying, but speaks almost perfect English.

"Olivia," he whispers to me while eyeing both men, and the machine gun. "What did you say to them?"

"Nothing, I swear." My palms are sweaty and I'm dying to take off my sweater

---

1 Excuse me?
2 What was that?
3 Yes, Leni with an *e* and *i.*

but don't want to cause more of a stir. Finally, the men stop talking. The man with the gun hands me back my papers.

"*No, es un* i,"[1] he says, pointing at the *i*. "*Leni*."

"My mistake," I say, with a smile, and move on past the guards and officially into the country.

THE SPANISH ALPHABET

First, the basics. Here's how you say the Spanish letters of the alphabet. Practice each one out loud.

a	(ah)	b	(beh)	c	(she)
d	(deh)	e	(eh)	f	(EH-feh)
g	(heh)	h	(AH-cheh)	i	(ee)
j	(HO-tah)	k	(kah)	l	(EL-leh)
m	(EM-meh)	n	(EN-neh)	ñ	(EH-nyeh)
o	(oh)	p	(peh)	q	(koo)
r	(HER-reh)	rr	(trilled r)	s	(EHS-seh)
t	(tay)	u	(oo)	v	(veh)
w	(DOH-bleh veh)	x	(EH-kees)	y	(EE gree-EH-grah)
z	(SEH-tah)				

Spanish also has the double letters *ch (cheh)* and *ll (EHL-yeh)*, but they are not officially part of the alphabet.

Olivia should have spelled-out her name *L (EL-leh)*, *A (ah)*, *N (EN-neh)*, *E (eh)*. The customs agent heard the English pronunciation of the letter *a*, and thought it was *e*. The same goes for the letter *e*, which the agent confused with *i*.

---

1   No, it is an *i*.

VOWEL SOUNDS

Vowels are hard to master in any language. Luckily, Spanish mostly looks the way it sounds, so you won't get any surprises like you do in English. Consider this: In English, *rough*, *dough*, and *thought* all have the same combination of letters but are pronounced differently. This would never happen in Spanish. However, the Spanish vowels are challenging all the same.

FORGET YOUR ENGLISH!

Now try to forget what you know in English and practice saying these Spanish sounds.

a: pronounced *ah*, as in the English word *yacht*		
casa	(*CAH-sah*)	(house)
gato	(*GAH-toh*)	(cat)
balde	(*BAHL-deh*)	(bucket)
e: pronounced eh, as in the English word *ten*		
bebé	(*beh-BEH*)	(baby)
sartén	(*sahr-TEHN*)	(frying pan)
tenedor	(*teh-neh-DOHR*)	(fork)
i: pronounced ee, as in the English word *year*		
libro	(*LEE-broh*)	(book)
silla	(*SEE-yah*)	(chair)
comida	(*coh-MEE-dah*)	(food)
o: pronounced oh, as in the English word *door*		
flor	(*flohr*)	(flower)
vaso	(*VAH-soh*)	(cup)
oro	(*OH-roh*)	(gold)
u: pronounced oo, as in the English word *moon*		
duro	(*DOO-roh*)	(hard)
atún	(*ah-TOON*)	(tuna)
punta	(*POON-tah*)	(point)

DIPHTHONGS

Diptongos, or **diphthongs**, are vowel combinations. Diphthongs are made up of a weak vowel and a strong vowel that both belong in the same syllable. *I* and *u* are considered weak vowels, and *a*, *e*, and *o* are strong vowels. When you see a diphthong, accent the strong vowel.

Consider, for example, the word *cuando* (when). The *u* is weak and the *a* is strong. Pronounce it as *(KOOAHN-doh)*.

You may ask, "What happens if I see two weak vowels?" Well, simply stress the second one.

| Suiza | *(SOOEE-sah)* | (Switzerland) |

If you see two strong vowels, separate them into their own syllables.

| feo | (FEH-oh) | (ugly) |

FORGET ENGLISH! THINK SPANISH!

In English, when vowels are combined, they may develop into a totally new sound. This is not quite the case in Spanish. For example, you might be inclined to pronounce the word *Europa* as *(yur-OH-pah)*, as you would in English. We'll say it again: Try to forget your English pronunciation for a moment. The correct pronunciation is *(ehoo-ROH-pah)*.

CONSONANT SOUNDS

Now that you've learned the vowels, the consonants will be a piece of cake. Most of them are pronounced just like in English. Here are the ones that are not.

b and v: pronounced like an English *b*		
banda	*(BAHN-dah)*	(band)
vida	*(VEE-dah)*	(life)
c: before *a*, *o*, and *u*, pronounced like an English *k*		
casa	*(CAH-sah)*	(house)

cosa	*(COH-sah)*	(thing)
cuna	*(COO-nah)*	(crib)

c: before *e* and *i*, pronounced like an English *s*

ceja	*(SEH-hah)*	(eyebrow)
cita	*(SEE-tah)*	(appointment)

g: before *a*, *o*, and *u*, pronounced like an English *g*

gracias	*(GRAH-seeahs)*	(thank you)
goma	*(GOH-mah)*	(glue)
guante	*(GOOAHN-teh)*	(glove)

g: before *e* and *i*, pronounced like an English *h*

gente	*(HEHN-teh)*	(people)
gitano	*(hee-TAH-noh)*	(gypsy)

g: before *ui* or *ue*, pronounced like an English *g*

guía	*(GHEE-ah)*	(guide)
guerra	*(GHE-rrah)*	(war)

h: Shhhh! It's silent!

hada	*(AH-dah)*	(fairy)
hecho	*(EH-choh)*	(fact)

j: pronounced like the English *h*

jardín	*(har-DEEN)*	(garden)
ají	*(ah-HEE)*	(hot sauce)

ñ: pronounced like the *ny* in *canyon*

piña	*(PEE-nyah)*	(pineapple)
año	*(AH-nyoh)*	(year)

q: preceding *ue* or *ui*, pronounced like the English *k*

queso	*(KEH-soh)*	(cheese)
aquí	*(ah-KEE)*	(here)

s and z: pronounced like an English *s*

sueño	*(SOOEH-nyoh)*	(sleepiness)
zapato	*(sah-PAH-toh)*	(shoe)

DOUBLE CONSONANTS

Spanish has two double consonants that are considered single letters: *ll* and *rr*.

Try to remember to pronounce them correctly, or you may confuse Spanish speakers. For example, the word *caro* (expensive) is pronounced differently than the word *carro* (car).

ll: pronounced like an English *y*		
llave	*(YAH-veh)*	(key)
olla	*(OH-yah)*	(pot)
rr: a heavily rolled *r*		
arroz	*(ah-RROHS)*	(rice)
horror	*(oh-RROHR)*	(horror)

STRESS

If you don't see an accent mark on the word, the stress will either be on the last or second-to-last syllable of the word.

Spanish speakers usually stress the last syllable of a word that ends in a consonant other than *n* or *s*.

papel	*(pah-PEL)*	(paper)
actriz	*(ahk-TREES)*	(actress)

If the last syllable of the word ends in an *n*, *s*, or vowel, the second-to-last syllable is stressed.

casa	*(CAH-sah)*	(house)
aroma	*(ah-ROH-mah)*	(aroma)

If you do see an accent mark, then stress the vowel that is accented.

camión	*(cah-MEEOHN)*	(truck)
sábado	*(SAH-bah-doh)*	(Saturday)

Now you've learned just about everything you need to know about pronunciation and stress in Spanish. When you're done reviewing, try the exercises at the end of the chapter.

YOUR TURN

The following Spanish words have underlined sounds. Try matching them to their English equivalents. Write the letter in the space provided.

1.	llama _____	a.	moon
2.	niño _____	b.	cat
3.	cine _____	c.	canyon
4.	ángel _____	d.	sleep
5.	uva _____	e.	door
6.	inca _____	f.	get
7.	cama _____	g.	sit
8.	amor _____	h.	yes
9.	flecha _____	i.	help
10.	gorra _____	j.	met

Look back over the rules of stress in Spanish. Now select which syllable has the correct stress, based on what you've learned. Write the letter in the space provided.

11. pájaro _____
    (A) pá JA ro (B) PÁ ja ro (C) pá ja RO

12. juvenil _____
    (A) JU ve nil (B) ju ve NIL (C) ju VE nil

13. naranja _____
    (A) NA ran ja (B) na ran JA (C) na RAN ja

14. canciones _____
    (A) can CION es (B) CAN cion es (C) can cion ES

15. corazón _____
    (A) co RA zón (B) CO ra zón (C) co ra ZÓN

2

CHAPTER 2
COGNATES

The *imigración* part of the airport is air-conditioned.[1] The rest of the place is not. This is the first thing I notice as I walk out and look around the *aeropuerto*.[2] Tons of people are waiting for their friends and loved ones to walk off the plane. Me, I'm looking for a bunch of strangers whom I've never set eyes on before. Soon, the rest of my group is out in the hot, humid air as well. I witness numerous greetings between students and host families, as the institute has printed each of our names on a large poster board that each of us carried off the plane. (At least *Lane* is spelled correctly there.)

After ten minutes it's clear that my host family is not among the families in the waiting room. Blair is chatting away with her family a few yards away and I see them all embrace her and compliment her on her Spanish. Andrés finally comes up to me.

"Olivia," he says.

"Yes," I say.

"The Capelos, your host family, called and left a message on my cell phone. It seems their son is flying back from his university this afternoon as well, so they've gone to pick him up at the national terminal and will be over shortly to pick you up. You don't mind waiting, do you?"

"Of course not," I say. What else am I supposed to say?

"Great," he says, and soon he's back in among the rest of the crowd.

After an hour, the luggage has been collected, cars have been brought around, and the crowd has dispersed. Everyone on my program is now with his or her family. Everyone except me, however, as my family has yet to show up. I sit down on my suitcase, still holding the stupid sign with my name on it. I doubt they'll have trouble spotting me now.

I look at my watch and sigh. I'm missing *Passions* right this minute. The air-

---

1   immigration
2   airport

port lounge *does* have a TV, but of course it's playing some weird Spanish show. The show seems to be set about two hundred years ago in some fancy mansion, and the one character I see is in a period costume—a chambermaid's outfit. The production values are pretty low, and the woman, a blonde, is overacting. She's sitting alone in a room, staring into a crystal ball with this wild look in her eyes. An image starts to appear in the ball of a beautiful brunette in a fancy gown, with this big, dark-colored gem hanging from a chain around her neck. The camera focuses in closer and closer on the gem, as the blonde laughs maniacally. *Ay caramba.*

At almost exactly the two-hour mark, a car pulls up to the curb. Five people are crammed inside a tiny, ancient Volkswagen. The driver's door pops open and a middle-aged man with a paunch steps out and stands by the car.

"*¿Hola?*" the man yells out.

"Uh, yes?" I say.

"*¿Olivia?*" he calls.

"That's me." I nod my head

"*Pues yo soy Señor Capelos. ¡Beinvenida a Costa Rica! ¡Vamos!*"[1] He gets back into the card and closes the door. I look around, pick up my suitcases, and drag them toward the car. Everyone inside the car seems to be talking at once. I try to open the trunk without much success. Finally, one of the back doors opens, and a guy who looks to be about twenty gets out.

"*Hola,*" he says. "*Me llamo Ernesto. Yo soy tu hermano Tico.*"[2]

"Uhh . . ." All I can do is nod. This guy is gorgeous. I mean, a total hunk. Then again, he's also the reason I've spent the past two hours alone sitting on my suitcase in a strange Latin American airport. With the bags inside, he motions me around to the other side of the car. I open the passenger door and see approximately three inches of seat space for me to sit in.

"*¡Vamos Olivia!*"[3] Señor yells with a laugh. Salsa music blasts from the radio. There's nothing else to do but push in. We're moving even before I've closed my door all the way. Now I'm riding with half my butt on the armrest on the door and the other half up against one of my new host sisters, I try to follow their rapid conversation in Spanish. I catch words here and there, but only those that sound like English. Soon,

---

1 Well, I am Señor Capelos. Welcome to Costa Rica! Let's go!

2 Hello. My name is Ernesto. I am your Costa Rican brother. (Costa Ricans use the term *tico* or *tica* to refer to themselves and their fellow compatriots.)

3 Let's go, Olivia!

some sort of argument starts between Ernesto and one of his sisters.

"*¡Por favor, no me molestes!*"[1] the younger girl says to Ernesto. I raise my eyebrows. Did she say "molest"? Maybe they aren't brother and sister after all.

"*Cállate o voy a molestarte cuando llegamos a la casa.*"[2] Señor barks from the front seat, practically yelling over the radio. Now, I'm not exactly sure what he just said, but it sounded an awful lot like he was going to start molesting people when we got home. I tense up immediately. Who are these people? Now being left alone at the airport for two hours seems like child's play.

USE WHAT YOU ALREADY KNOW

Learning a language isn't easy. You know that. But this chapter will prove that you've known a little Spanish your whole life! Tackle each word at a time, and you'll realize that you know more than you think.

Of course, it's obvious: If you know how to add, apply that to your math problems. If you know how to scramble an egg, apply that to your cooking. Take advantage of the skills you already know to get ahead in life. Do the same with Spanish.

COGNATES

Many Spanish words resemble words in other languages and have identical or similar meanings. These words are called **cognates**. The more languages you study, the more cognates you'll recognize. If you've studied French, Italian, or Portuguese, you know what we mean. Because of their roots in Latin, the Romance languages have many similarities.

Since English and Spanish share a common heritage in Latin, you will see similar words. There are only minor differences in spelling between English and Spanish cognates.

---

1 Please, don't bother me!
2 Be quiet, or I'm going to bother you when we get to the house!

Take a look at the following words. Can you figure out what they mean?

estación   increíble   paciencia

If you're catching on, you'll agree that the words are *station*, *incredible*, and *patience*.

LOOK FOR PATTERNS

Cognates are easy to spot because they look just like English words. Look for patterns too. Once you learn these patterns, you'll be able to recognize new words.

-ción	-tion	-oso/a	-ous
imigración	immigration	famoso	famous
sensación	sensation	religiosa	religious
-dad	-ty	-cia	-ce
curiosidad	curiosity	agencia	agency
identidad	identity	esencia	essence

Many of the names of school subjects in Spanish and English come from the same Latin or Greek roots.

-ica	-ics	-ía	-y
matemática	mathematics	historia	history
física	physics	filosofía	philosophy

COGNATE ADJECTIVES

Take a look at the words below. They are all cognate adjectives that can be used to describe either a male or a female. They do not change form in the singular.

excelente	difícil	egoísta	feminista	idealista
indiferente	intelectual	inteligente	interesante	materialista
natural	horrible	popular	responsable	sentimental

Now take a look at these words. They are cognate adjectives that change form in the singular. Use *-o* to describe a male and *-a* to describe a female.

agresivo/a	famoso/a	generoso/a
impulsivo/a	nervioso/a	honesto/a
romántico/a	sincero/a	tímido/a

WATCH OUT FOR FALSE FRIENDS!

We just saw that if a Spanish word looks like an English word it probably means the same thing. However, some words are wolves in sheeps' clothing. Words that look similar but have different meanings are called **false friends**.

What do you think the word *librería* means? "Library"? Gotcha! No, it actually means "bookstore." *Biblioteca* means "library." Here's another false friend: *embarazada*. It actually means "pregnant." If you want to say that you're embarrassed, the adjective is *avergonzado/a*.

Here are some more false friends:

carpeta: folder (*not* carpet)
campo: field or countryside (*not* camping)
compromiso: engagement or obligation (*not* compromise)
contestar: to answer (*not* to contest)
éxito: success (*not* exit)
fábrica: factory (*not* fabric)
molestar: to bother (*not* to molest)
recordar: to remember (*not* to record)
ropa: clothes (*not* rope)
sopa: soup (*not* soap)
tuna: cactus fruit (*not* tuna fish)

Moral of the story: If you ever have a doubt as to whether or not a word is a cognate, the best thing to do is look it up in the dictionary.

CROSSOVER WORDS

What's a crossover word? Well, have you heard about Hispanic singers "crossing over" to the English world? Singers like Ricky Martin, Enrique Iglesias, and Gloria Estefan all started their careers by singing in Spanish. At some point, these bilingual stars decided to expand their fan base by singing in English too. Well, **crossover words**, as you can imagine, are English words that have entered the Spanish language and vice versa.

There are many examples of Spanish words being absorbed into the English language. Consider the following words.

fiesta	mañana	señorita	siesta	tango

There are also examples of English being absorbed into Spanish. Look at these words. See, you *do* know some Spanish!

| hamburguesa | suéter | sándwich |

Crossover influence makes each language richer. Ricky Martin and Enrique Iglesias crossed over for a reason: They wanted to reach more people. They certainly were successful.

YOUR TURN

Can you figure out the Spanish equivalents of the following words?

1. sensation
2. depression
3. pessimism
4. invention
5. celebration
6. curious
7. urgent
8. prosperity
9. experience
10. optimism

Identify the following cognates by giving their English equivalents.

11. geografía
12. artista
13. farmacia
14. nación
15. fabuloso
16. paradiso
17. humanidad
18. dormitorio
19. profesor
20. museo

3

CHAPTER 3
SENTENCES AND QUESTIONS

The drive from the airport out to the Capelos' house in Escazu is nothing short of thrilling, not necessarily for the views or the city itself, but because everything is so different. There are cars and trucks and highways and road signs, but they are all strange, the same yet completely different from the ones we have back in New York. The Capelos' town, Escazu, is in the hills outside San José. We pull up under a small carport next to a one-story house on a narrow road. The neighborhood is quiet on this Monday night. We all go inside, and I'm shown to my room, which I share with the two girls.

With a little quick dictionary sleuthing, the whole *molestar* thing is swept under the rug. However, I'm less inclined to let Ernesto off that easily. I mean, you should see how this guy is treated. He's the king of the house! Whatever he wants, he gets. Well, I'm not particularly interested in any of this macho nonsense, even if he is drop-dead gorgeous. When he walks into the kitchen, everyone's running around trying to get him stuff. When he goes into the living room, whoever has the remote for the TV hands it to him. It's really kind of annoying. Apart from that, though, it feels really good to be in the Capelos' house.

Now, we all have certain rituals in life that we kind of depend on, and one of mine is a glass of fresh squeezed orange juice right when I get out of bed in the morning. On the drive here I noticed beautiful, fragrant groves of orange trees, so I figure this shouldn't pose much of a problem. I decide to bring this up first thing after I unpack.

"Hello?" I say as I walked into the kitchen. "I mean, um, *¿Hola?*"

"*¿Hola?*" My host mother, whom I call Señora, calls out "*¿Olivia? ¿Qué necesitas?*"[1]

---

1   Olivia? What do you need?

"Um, yeah," I said. "*¿Mañana?*[1] May I please have some orange juice?" I get a blank stare in response. Um, right. "*¿Mañana?*"

"*Sí, mañana,*" Señora says.

"*Por favor, yo quiero* orange juice.[2] In the morning." Still no response. Then Ernesto walks in. I repeat some of what I said before, but Ernesto is puzzled, too.

"*¿Tienes sed?*"[3] Ernesto says, walking over to the refrigerator.

"Um, *¿que?*" Ernesto starts pouring me a glass of water.

"*¿No tienes sed?*"

"Um, not now. I mean, no. *No sed. Pero en la mañana,*[4] I'd like some orange juice."

"*¿No tienes sed?*" he asks.

"No. Um, *en la mañana, sí. Sed.*"[5]

"*Ah, entiendo,*"[6] Ernesto says, then says something to his mother. They both look at me and smile.

Well, that was easy. Señora and Ernesto understand my needs. I've successfully communicated what I need, in Spanish. The next twenty-nine days will be a breeze.

FORMING SENTENCES

First, let's learn a little about forming sentences. We need to start with the basics.

SENTENCE COMPONENTS

You learn this in your grammar class every year, but here are the basic components of a sentence and their functions. You will learn more about each in later chapters.

---

1 Tomorrow?
2 Please, I would like . . .
3 Are you thirsty?
4 Not thirsty. But in the morning
5 In the morning, yes. Thirst.
6 Oh, I understand.

1. *sustantivo* (noun): a person, place, or thing

botella	(bottle)
perros	(dogs)

2. *verbo* (verb): an action or state

comer	(to eat)
ser	(to be)

3. *artículo* (article): accompanies and identifies a noun

el libro	(**the** book)
una muñeca	(**a** doll)

4. *adjetivo* (adjective): modifies a noun

la silla **roja**	(the **red** chair)
el niño **bueno**	(the **good** boy)

5. *adverbio* (adverb): modifies a verb, adjective, or another adverb

Marta habla **bien**.	(Marta speaks **well**.)
La mujer camina **lentamente**.	(The woman walks **slowly**.)

6. *pronombre* (pronoun): replaces a noun

Isabel tiene trece años.	(Isabel is thirteen years old.)
Ella tiene trece años.	(**She** is thirteen years old.)

7. *preposición* (preposition): expresses the relationship between things in terms of time or place

El vaso está **en** la mesa.	(The glass is **on** the table.)
Te veo **antes de** las 3:00.	(See you **before** 3:00.)

Now that we've reviewed the basics, let's learn how to form a complete sentence.

SUBJECT AND PREDICATE

In Spanish, as in English, a sentence is formed by combining a subject and a verb, or predicate.

The **subject** is the person or thing that we are talking about, generally a noun. The **predicate** is everything else. The predicate can describe a quality or an action. It contains the verb.

Take a look at the following sentences, in English, before you move on to the Spanish examples.

The cat is playing with the toy mouse.

Teddy's mom is the school nurse.

Now look at these sentences in Spanish. Try to identify the subjects and the predicates.

Mi amigo Daniel está muy feliz.	(My friend Daniel is very happy.)
Los muchachos están en la cocina.	(The boys are in the kitchen.)
La hermana de Catalina es inteligente.	(Catalina's sister is intelligent.)

As you can see, both the subject and the predicate can contain more than one word. In the sentences, the subjects are *mi amigo Daniel*, *los muchachos*, and *la hermana de Catalina*. The predicates are *está muy feliz*, *están en la cocina*, and *es inteligente*.

You can also see that, in Spanish, the subject generally comes first, then the verb, then the adjective or object (if there is one).

SUBJECT-VERB AGREEMENT

In Spanish, each verb tense has a specific ending that agrees with the subject in person and in number. There are six possible endings for each verb—three singular and three plural. You'll learn more about verbs in Chapter 5.

Remember that the predicate is everything we say about the subject. The predicate must have at least one word. This word, a verb, should agree in person and number with the subject.

In this example, *canta* agrees in number with *Carla* (both are singular). Flip over to Chapter 5 if you want to learn the rest of the verb endings. But for now, trust us. The verb has to agree with the subject, and in this case, it does.

subject   predicate
Carla canta.   (Carla sings.)

In this example, *cantan* agrees in number with *las niñas*. Both are plural.

subject   predicate
Las niñas cantan.   (The girls sing.)

Interestingly, in Spanish, sentences can be made up of a single, conjugated verb because it includes both concepts: subject and predicate. As you know, this is not the case in English.

Canta.   (He/She sings.)
Cantan.   (They sing.)

FORMING QUESTIONS

Now that you know how to form a sentence, you can form a question. There are several ways of doing it.

One way is to add a tag at the end of the sentence.

sentence: María habla español.   (María speaks Spanish.)
question: María habla español, ¿no?   (María speaks Spanish, doesn't she?)

Another way to ask a question is to invert, or switch the placement of, the subject and the verb. The word order will generally be: *verb + rest of predicate (if any) + subject*. Spanish is pretty flexible. As long as the verb comes first, it generally doesn't matter which noun comes next.

sentence: María habla español.   (María speaks Spanish.)
question: ¿Habla español María?   (Does María speak Spanish?)
question: ¿Habla María español?

A third way is to change the intonation of the sentence. Simply make the sentence a question. However, this is the least common way of asking a question. Be careful if you choose to use it, because it can result in miscommunication.

sentence: María habla español.   (María speaks Spanish.)
question: ¿María habla español?   (María speaks Spanish?)

QUESTION WORDS

Like in English, questions in Spanish often begin with question words. Here are some question words, or *palabras interrogativas*.

¿Qué?	What?	**¿Cuándo**?	When?
¿Quién?	Who?	**¿Cuánto/a**?	How much?
¿Quiénes?	Who?	**¿Cuántos/as**?	How many?

¿Cuál?	Which one?	¿Dónde?	Where?
¿Cuáles?	Which ones?	¿Adónde?	To where?
		¿De dónde?	From where?
¿Cómo?	How?	¿Por qué?	Why?

Now take a look at how question words are used.

¿Qué quieres?	What do you want?
¿Quién es?	Who is it?
¿Quiénes son?	Who are they?
¿Cuál es tu libro?	Which one is your book?
¿Cuáles son tus libros?	Which ones are your books?
¿Cómo tomas el café?	How do you take your coffee?
¿Cuándo vamos al teatro?	When are we going to the theater?
¿Cuánta leche quieres?	How much milk do you want?
¿Cuántas manzanas quieres?	How many apples do you want?
¿Dónde está el carro?	Where is the car?
¿Adónde vas?	Where are you going?
¿De dónde eres?	Where are you from?
¿Por qué gritas?	Why are you yelling?

¿Cuál? and *¿cuáles?* are often used to choose from among a group of things. For example, in the following sentences, it is assumed that there are several books to choose from.

¿Cuál es tu libro? (Which one is your book?)
¿Cuáles son tus libros? (Which ones are your books?)

ANSWERING QUESTIONS

You've learned how to ask a question. Now let's go over how to answer a question.

If the question asked is a yes/no question, this is how you can answer it.

¿Vas al cine? (Are you going to the cinema?)

| Sí, voy. | (Yes, I am going.) |
| No, no voy. | (No, I'm not going.) |

When a question contains a question word, this is how you can answer it.

¿Cuándo es la fiesta?	(When is the party?)
Es a las 5:00.	(It's at 5:00.)
¿Por qué estás triste?	(Why are you sad?)
Porque no tengo amigos.	(Because I don't have any friends.)
¿Quién es?	(Who is it?)
Es mi madre.	(It's my mother.)

When answering questions, pay attention to the verb form. The verb form in the answer will be based on the one in the question. If the question is asked of *you*, for example, the answer is in the *I* form. If the question is asked about *him*, the answer is about *him*. Here's how it works.

If the question is about *yo*, answer it with *tú* or *usted*.

| ¿Cuándo voy al colegio? | (When am I going to school?) |
| Vas a las 8:00. | (You're going at 8:00.) |

If the question is about *tú* or *usted*, answer it with *yo*.

| ¿Cuándo va usted al colegio? | (When are you going to school?) |
| Voy a las 8:00. | (I'm going at 8:00.) |

If the question is about *nosotros*, answer it with *nosotros*.

| ¿Cuándo vamos al colegio? | (When are we going to school?) |
| Vamos a las 8:00. | (We're going at 8:00.) |

If the question is about *ellos*, answer it with *ellos*.

| ¿Cuándo van al colegio? | (When are they going to school?) |
| Van a las 8:00 | (They're going at 8:00.) |

Finally, if the question is about *ustedes*, answer it with *nosotros*.

| ¿Cuándo van ustedes al colegio? | (When are you going to school?) |
| Vamos a las 8:00. | (We're going at 8:00.) |

Now we've covered sentences and questions. When you're done reviewing, try the exercises at the end of the chapter.

YOUR TURN

Identify the subjects and predicates of the following sentences. Circle the subjects, and underline the predicates.

1. Martín está en la cocina.
2. Anita tiene zapatos negros.
3. Yo soy de los Estados Unidos.
4. Los ojos de Antonieta son azules.
5. La computadora es nueva.
6. Miguel tiene tres hermanos.
7. Usted es muy inteligente.
8. Nosotros vamos a la fiesta.
9. El teatro es bonito.
10. Tu hermano está en México.

Choose the correct question to agree with each answer. Write the letter in the space provided.

11. Sí, hablo español. _____
    (A) ¿Quién habla español? (B) ¿Hablas español?

12. No, Alberto no está aquí. _____
    (A) ¿Dónde está Alberto? (B) Alberto no está aquí, ¿verdad?

13. Soy de Nueva York. _____
    (A) ¿De dónde es usted? (B) ¿De dónde es Raúl?

14. Necesito un lápiz. _____
    (A) ¿Cuáles lapices necesitas? (B) ¿Qué necesitas?

15. Porque es mi amiga. _____
    (A) ¿Dónde está Marta? (B) ¿Por qué hablas con Marta?

CHAPTER 4
NOUNS AND ARTICLES

The next morning, I leap out of my *cama*,[1] change quickly, and walk into the kitchen, hoping for that nice fresh glass of orange juice. Everyone is there and, as usual, talking a mile a minute. Everyone except Ernesto.

"*Hola,* Olivia," Señora says, taking my hand and leading me to a seat at the table. "*¿Qué quieres?*"[2]

Hmmm. Didn't we sort this out last night?

"Um, orange juice?" I say, but she doesn't follow. *Juice,* how do you say *juice?* Just then, Ernesto strolls out of his room. He's carrying a pitcher of what appears to be freshly squeezed orange juice.

"Oh, *hola,* Olivia," Ernesto says, pulling up a chair next to me. "*¿Cómo estás?*"[3] He pours well over half the pitcher into his glass on the table. Then he picks up the glass and drinks the entire thing in one gulp.

"*Hola,*" I mumble, unable to take my eyes off his now empty glass. Then my two Costa Rican sisters come bounding in. One of them grabs the pitcher from Ernesto; before I can say a thing, she pours the rest of the juice into a glass, drinks half of it, and then gives the glass to her sister, who drinks the other half. Ernesto looks at me and starts to yell at his sisters, but it is too late. The orange juice is gone. I get up and head to my room. I've got to change and head to class, anyway.

NOUNS

Years of grammar classes have drilled into your head that a **noun** is a person, place, or thing. Same thing goes in Spanish, but there are a few additions.

---

1 bed
2 What would you like?
3 How are you?

GENDER

You know what gender means from science class. **Gender** means "male" or "female." Now apply that concept to nouns: Spanish nouns can be masculine or feminine. Yep, it's true. Think of them as boy nouns and girl nouns.

There is no real rule for determining the gender of a Spanish noun. Eventually you'll figure them all out. But there are certain indicators you can look for before you actually reach fluency in the language.

WORD ENDING: MASCULINE

The easiest way to determine the gender of a Spanish noun is to look at how it ends.

So far, so good, right? Now, before you carve any of the following rules in stone, remember this: In any language, there are exceptions. In fact, at times there are so many exceptions that you have to wonder why a rule was made at all.

Most nouns that end in -o are masculine.

el perro	(the dog)
el libro	(the book)

EXCEPTIONS: The following nouns are all feminine, even though they end in -o.

la mano	(the hand)
la radio	(the radio)
la moto	(the motorcycle)
la foto	(the photograph)

Most nouns that end in -l or -r are masculine.

el barril	(the barrel)
el actor	(the actor)

EXCEPTIONS: The following nouns are all feminine, even though they end in -l.

la capital	(the capital)
la miel	(the honey)
la piel	(the skin)
la sal	(the salt)

Most nouns that end in –aje are masculine.

el garaje	(the garage)

el personaje	(the character)

WORD ENDING: FEMININE
Most nouns that end in -*a* are feminine.

la casa	(the house)
la mesa	(the table)

EXCEPTIONS: The following nouns are all masculine, even though they end in -*a*.

el día	(the day)
el poema	(the poem)
el planeta	(the planet)
el idioma	(the language)

Most nouns that end in -*ad*, -*ción*, -*sión*, -*umbre*, and -*ud* are feminine. Some of these words are cognates of English.

la libertad	(the liberty)
la condición	(the condition)
la decisión	(the decision)
la costumbre	(the custom)
la salud	(the health)

WORD ENDING: BOTH FEMININE AND MASCULINE
Some nouns in Spanish can be feminine or masculine. Look for the -*ista* ending.

el/la artista	(the artist)
el/la turista	(the tourist)
el/la pianista	(the pianist)

MEANING: FEMININE AND MASCULINE
Another way of determining whether a noun is masculine or feminine is to think about what the word means.

If a noun refers to a male, it will be masculine.

el rey	(the king)
el león	(the lion)

If a noun refers to a female, it will be feminine.

la actriz	(the actress)
la vaca	(the cow)

Many masculine nouns that end in *-o* change to *-a* to form the feminine.

el tío/la tía	(the aunt/the uncle)
el hijo/la hija	(the son/the daughter)

NUMBER

Now that you can identify the gender of a noun, you should learn how to form the plural. Actually, there's not much to learn. Simply follow these rules.

If a noun ends in a vowel, form the plural by adding *-s*.

el gato	los gatos	(the cat/the cats)
la pluma	las plumas	(the pen/the pens)

If a noun ends in a consonant, form the plural by adding *-es*.

la ciudad	las ciudades	(the city/the cities)
el reloj	los relojes	(the watch/the watches)

DEFINITE ARTICLES

You probably noticed that all the nouns discussed thus far have been accompanied by the words *el*, *la*, *los*, or *las*. These are **definite articles**. Their English equivalent is *the*. Definite articles point out something in particular. For example, in the phrase *the house*, the *the* points out a particular house.

Try to learn nouns with their articles. This will help you remember whether they are masculine or feminine.

As you can imagine, feminine nouns are accompanied by the feminine definite article. Masculine nouns are accompanied by the masculine definite article.

	Singular	Plural
masculine	el	los
feminine	la	las

There is one exception to the rule. (In Spanish there are sometimes more exceptions than rules.) When the definite article comes before a feminine word that begins with *a* or *ha*, the singular masculine article is used. You can probably guess why if you say it out loud–Spanish, being a particularly melodious language, will not accept the double "a" sound.

el hacha (*not* la hacha)   las hachas   (the axes/the axes)

Say *la agua* out loud and you'll see what we are talking about. With the plural, you can use the "right" article, as the *s* in *las* breaks up that double "a" sound.

INDEFINITE ARTICLES

The indefinite articles *un*, *una*, *unos*, and *unas* are equivalent to the English indefinite articles *a*, *an*, and *some*. The indefinite article refers to something in general. For example, in the phrase *a house*, the *a* refers to a general (that is, not specific) house.

	Singular	Plural
masculine	un	unos
feminine	una	unas

In Spanish, indefinite articles follow the same rules as the definite articles: When the indefinite article comes before a feminine word that begins with *a* or *ha*, the singular masculine article is used.

un agua   unas aguas   (a water/some waters)
un hacha   unas hachas   (an axe/some axes)

YOUR TURN

Use what you've learned about gender to decide which definite article accompanies each noun. Write the article in the space provided.

1. _____ mano
2. _____ mesa
3. _____ piel
4. _____ personaje
5. _____ agua
6. _____ actriz
7. _____ niño
8. _____ rey
9. _____ hija
10. _____ artista

Change each definite article to an indefinite article. Rewrite the entire phrase in the space provided.

11. las nueces_____
12. el águila _____
13. los mapas _____
14. la pluma _____
15. las fotos _____

Now change each indefinite article to a definite article. Rewrite the entire phrase in the space provided.

16. un garaje _____
17. una decisión _____
18. unos relojes _____
19. un barril _____
20. unas motos _____

5

CHAPTER 5
REGULAR VERBS
(PRESENT TENSE)

"*Hola, clase,*" Profesor says. "*En esta clase yo no quiero oír ninguna palabra en inglés. Sólo español. ¿Me entiendes?*"[1]

"*Sí, Profesor,*" everyone, except for me, answers in unison. What, did they practice that in Spanish Club?

"*¿Sabe Ud. el verbo hablar?*"[2] he says, pointing at me.

"*Sí,*" I say.

"*Bueno. Entonces por favor escriba las formas corectas del verbo en el presente.*"[3] He has his hand out, extending the chalk to me. I feel the eyes of the entire class on me.

"Um," I say. My mind is a complete blank. Of all the kids in the class, he had to pick me to go first.

"*¿Perdóname?*"[4]

I lower my eyes to my desk. The silence is deadly. Profesor finally moves on. And it wasn't like I didn't know what he was asking. As soon as the next kid starts to say it, I realize I knew the conjugation.

---

1   Hello, class. In this class I don't want to hear a word of English. Only Spanish. Do you understand me?

2   Do you know the verb *hablar* (to speak)?

3   Good. Therefore, please write the correct forms of the verb in the present tense.

4   Excuse me?

VERBS

In Chapter 3, we explained that a **verb** is a state or action.

Carol eats breakfast every day.   (*eats* expresses an action)
Daniel is in a good mood.   (*is* expresses a state)

Spanish verbs all end with one of three letter combinations: *-ar*, *-er*, or *-ir*.

cantar	(to sing)
comer	(to eat)
escribir	(to write)

There are both regular and irregular verbs with all three endings. Regular verbs all conjugate in the same way. When you conjugate a verb, you form different tenses (past, present, future) and persons (*I, you, he, she, it, we, they*). Once you learn how to conjugate a regular verb, you can conjugate all verbs like it in the same way. Irregular verbs are a little trickier, but we're not getting to those until Chapter 7.

SUBJECT PRONOUNS

Before we get too immersed in Spanish verbs, let's review subject pronouns. A **pronoun** replaces a noun in a sentence. A **subject pronoun**, therefore, replaces a noun that is a subject.

Andrew likes hamburgers. **He** likes hamburgers.

Margaret and Suzy are going to the store. **They** are going to the store.

Here are the Spanish subject pronouns. Learn them now, because you will see them throughout the rest of the book. Note that there is no equivalent for the English *it*.

For the singular:

Person		
1st	yo	I
2nd	tú	you
3rd	él	he
	ella	she
	usted	you (formal)

For the plural:

Person		
1st	nosotros	we (masculine)
	nosotras	we (feminine)
2nd	vosotros	you (masculine)
	vosotras	you (feminine)
3rd	ellos	they (masculine)
	ellas	they (feminine)
	ustedes	you (formal)

Spanish has four subject pronouns that mean *you*. Here are the rules:

Use *tú* to address someone informally, like a friend or someone younger.

Use *usted* to address someone formally, like a teacher, stranger, or older person.

Use *ustedes* to address two or more people formally or informally in Latin America. Use *ustedes* to address two or more people formally in Spain.

Use *vosotros/vosotras* to address two or more people informally in Spain.

Confusing, isn't it? A rule of thumb: If you plan on using your Spanish in Latin America, don't spend too much time fretting about the *vosotros* form. People don't use it at all and will look at you strangely if you do. If you're traveling in Spain, on the other hand, it would be wise to study the *vosotros* form. In both cases, you should at least be able to recognize it.

You should also know that *nosotros*, *vosotros*, and *ellos* can refer to either a group of men or a group of men and women. *Nosotras*, *vosotras*, and *ellas* can refer only to a group of women.

REGULAR VERBS

In all regular Spanish verbs, the first section of the word, or **stem**, stays the same when the verb is conjugated.

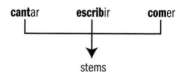

cantar   **escrib**ir   **com**er

stems

To form the present tense of a regular verb, first drop the infinitive ending: -ar, -er, or -ir, then add the correct endings to the stem. The verb with the infinitive ending means "to" + the action of the verb. *Comer* means "to eat." It is this form that is found in the dictionary.

-AR VERBS

For singular -ar verbs, add -o, -as, and -a.

Person		Singular
1st	yo canto	I sing
2nd	tú cantas	you sing
	él canta	he sings
3rd	ella canta	she sings
	usted canta	you sing (formal)

For plural -ar verbs, add -amos, -áis, and -an.

Person		Plural
1st	nosotros cantamos	we sing (masculine)
	nosotras cantamos	we sing (feminine)
2nd	vosotros cantáis	you sing (masculine)
	vosotras cantáis	you sing (feminine)

3rd	ellos cantan	they sing (masculine)
	ellas cantan	they sing (feminine)
	ustedes cantan	you sing (formal)

-*ER* VERBS

For singular -*er* verbs, add -*o*, -*es*, and -*e*.

Person	Singular	
1st	yo como	I eat
2nd	tú comes	you eat
3rd	él come	he eats
	ella come	she eats
	usted come	you eat (formal)

For plural -*er* verbs, add -*emos*, -*éis*, and -*en*.

Person	Plural	
1st	nosotros comemos	we eat (masculine)
	nosotras comemos	we eat (feminine)
2nd	vosotros coméis	you eat (masculine)
	vosotras coméis	you eat (feminine)
3rd	ellos comen	they eat (masculine)
	ellas comen	they eat (feminine)
	ustedes comen	you eat (formal)

-*IR* VERBS

For singular -*ir* verbs, add -*o*, -*es*, and -*e*.

Person	Singular	
1st	yo escribo	I write
2nd	tú escribes	you write
3rd	él escribe	he writes
	ella escribe	she writes
	usted escribe	you write (formal)

For plural *-ir* verbs, add *-imos*, *-ís*, and *-en.*

Person		Plural
1st	nosotros escribimos	we write (masculine)
	nosotras escribimos	we write (feminine)
2nd	vosotros escribís	you write (plural, masculine)
	vosotras escribís	you write (plural, feminine)
3rd	ellos escriben	they write (masculine)
	ellas escriben	they write (feminine)
	ustedes escriben	you write (plural, formal)

REVIEW: SUBJECT-VERB AGREEMENT

Back in Chapter 3, we explained that each verb must agree in person and number with its subject. Try to not forget this, both for Spanish and English. If you were to get the rule wrong in English, you might say, "I goes to the store," instead of "I go to the store." Doesn't sound very bright, does it? Well, you don't want to sound dumb in Spanish either.

We also said that a Spanish sentence can be made up of a single conjugated verb. Now that you've learned a little about regular verbs, you can see why this is possible. Unlike English, Spanish verb endings are each unique. In other words, you can generally tell who or what the subject is by simply looking at the verb ending. The subject or subject pronoun is used if you need to clarify the subject, or for emphasis.

All of the following examples are complete sentences.

Las niñas comen.	(The girls eat.)
Comen.	(They eat.)
Yo como.	(I eat.)
Como.	(I eat.)

Now you should be ready to practice what you've learned about regular verbs. Review the chapter and then try the following exercises.

YOUR TURN

Use what you learned to fill in the gaps in the following verb charts.

1. saludar (to greet)

Person	Singular	Plural
1st	yo _____	nosotros _____ nosotras saludamos
2nd	tú saludas	vosotros _____ vosotras saludáis
3rd	él saluda ella _____ usted saluda	ellos saludan ellas _____ ustedes saludan

2. _____ (to learn)

Person	Singular	Plural
1st	yo aprendo	nosotros aprendemos nosotras _____
2nd	tú _____	vosotros _____ vosotras _____
3rd	él _____ ella _____ usted aprende	ellos _____ ellas aprenden ustedes _____

Fill in the blanks with the correct form of the verb in parentheses.

3. Iris _____ (correr) en el parque.
4. Mis hermanas _____ (vivir) en Nueva York.
5. Yo _____ (abrir) el libro.
6. Vosotras _____ (estudiar) el español.
7. Tú _____ (comer) una pera.
8. Nosotros _____ (preparar) la comida.
9. Usted _____ (leer) la revista.
10. Ustedes _____ (escribir) una carta

11. Yo _____ (comprender) el ejercicio.
12. Vosotros _____ (regresar) a casa.

CHAPTER 6
OTHER REGULAR VERBS
(PRESENT TENSE)

When I get home from my first day of class, everyone in my host family is there, including Señor, home from work. The house is full of wonderful smells, and I'm starving. Everyone is talking, the radio and the TV are on, and Señor is sitting at the table in the middle of everything, reading the paper.

I think about the fact that I've never seen my own father at home at 1:30 on a Monday afternoon. We all sit down and have lunch, which is really dinner down here, the big meal of the day. The two sisters are talking back and forth, and Ernesto and his mother are discussing something. So I try and talk to Señor.

"Um, ¿perdóname?"[1]

"Sí, mi amor,"[2] Señor says.

"Yes, Señor? I was just wondering, ¿Qué haces?[3] I mean, do you work? I just can't remember the last time my father was at home during the day."

"Lo siento, ¿qué me preguntas? Dime en español."[4]

"Oh yeah, okay, so yo estudiar. Yo estudio y voy a la escuela. ¿Y tu?[5]

"Ah, entiendo," Señor says, laughing. "Sí, yo trabajo. Soy ingeniero. ¿Pero que piensas? ¿Piensas que yo no trabajo?"[6] And with that he turns back to his newspaper, indicating that the conversation is over. Okay, I think to myself. That went well.

---

1 Um, excuse me?
2 Yes, my love. ("My love" is a colloquialism used throughout Spanish-speaking countries).
3 What do you do?
4 I'm sorry. What are you asking me? Tell me in Spanish.
5 I study and got to school. And you?
6 Oh, I understand. Yes, I work. I am an engineer. But what did you think? Did you think I didn't have a job?

STEM-CHANGING VERBS

Just when you thought you were done with regular verbs . . . we present you with yet another kind: the **stem-changing verb**.

What happens when you conjugate a stem-changing verb? Well, as you can probably guess, the stem changes. This happens in all forms except *nosotros* and *vosotros*. But relax, the endings are all regular. In other words, you can apply the endings that you just learned in Chapter 5.

Take a look at the following types of stem-changing verbs.

E-IE

CERRAR (TO CLOSE)

Person	Singular	Plural
1st	yo cierro	nosotros cerramos
2nd	tú cierras	vosotros cerráis
3rd	él cierra	ellos cierran
	ella cierra	ellas cierran
	usted cierra	ustedes cierran

Other verbs like *cerrar*:

despertar	(to awaken)
empezar	(to begin)
pensar	(to think)
perder	(to lose)

Person	Singular	Plural
1st	yo pierdo	nosotros perdemos
2nd	tú pierdes	vosotros perdéis
3rd	él pierde	ellos pierden
	ella pierde	ellas pierden
	usted pierde	ustedes pierden

Other verbs like *perder*:

defender	(to defend)
entender	(to understand)
querer	(to want or love)

SENTIR (TO FEEL)

Person	Singular	Plural
1st	yo siento	nosotros sentimos
2nd	tú sientes	vosotros sentís
3rd	él siente	ellos sienten
	ella siente	ellas sienten
	usted siente	ustedes sienten

Other verbs like *sentir*:

mentir	(to lie)
divertir	(to amuse)
preferir	(to prefer)

E-I

PEDIR (TO REQUEST, TO ASK)

Person	Singular	Plural
1st	yo pido	nosotros pedimos
2nd	tú pides	vosotros pedís
3rd	él pide ella pide usted pide	ellos piden ellas piden ustedes piden

Other verbs like *pedir*:

repetir	(to repeat)
servir	(to serve)
vestir	(to dress)

O-UE

CONTAR (TO COUNT, TO TELL)

Person	Singular	Plural
1st	yo cuento	nosotros contamos
2nd	tú cuentas	vosotros contáis
3rd	él cuenta ella cuenta usted cuenta	ellos cuentan ellas cuentan ustedes cuentan

Other verbs like *contar*:

almorzar	(to have lunch)
costar	(to cost)
recordar	(to remember)

VOLVER (TO RETURN)

Person	Singular	Plural
1st	yo vuelvo	nosotros volvemos
2nd	tú vuelves	vosotros volvéis
3rd	él vuelve ella vuelve usted vuelve	ellos vuelven ellas vuelven ustedes vuelven

Other verbs like *volver*:

devolver	(to return)
llover	(to rain)
mover	(to move)

-UIR, -IAR, AND -UAR VERBS

Three more types of regular verbs in the present tense—we're almost done, so hang in there!

When conjugated, *-uir* verbs have a slight change in spelling in all forms except *nosotros* and *vosotros*: A *y* is added after the *u*. Take a look at the following chart.

INCLUIR (TO INCLUDE)

Person	Singular	Plural
1st	yo incluyo	nosotros incluimos
2nd	tú incluyes	vosotros incluís
3rd	él incluye ella incluye usted incluye	ellos incluyen ellas incluyen ustedes incluyen

Other verbs like *incluir*:

destruir	(to destroy)
distribuir	(to distribute)

Luckily, we're not going to make you learn any new endings or spellings for *-iar* and *-uar* verbs. The change is simply a matter of stress.

When you conjugate *-iar* verbs, stress the *i* in the singular and third-person plural. Take a look at the following chart.

ENVIAR (TO SEND)

Person	Singular	Plural
1st	yo envío	nosotros enviamos
2nd	tú envías	vosotros enviáis
3rd	él envía ella envía usted envía	ellos envían ellas envían ustedes envían

Other verbs like *enviar*:

confiar	(to trust in)
guiar	(to guide)

When you conjugate *-uar* verbs, stress the *u* in the singular and third-person plural. Take a look at the following chart.

ACTUAR (TO ACT)

Person	Singular	Plural
1st	yo actúo	nosotros actuamos
2nd	tú actúas	vosotros actuáis
3rd	él actúa ella actúa usted actúa	ellos actúan ellas actúan ustedes actúan

Other verbs like *actuar*:

continuar	(to continue)
graduarse	(to graduate)

Review the two verb charts we just presented. Did you notice the accent on the *i* and the *u*? If you think back to Chapter 1, you'll remember that these two vowels are considered to be weak. When a stressed weak vowel is paired with a strong vowel, it must have an accent mark.

You've learned just about all you need to know about that nebulous category of regular verbs that we call "other." Let's do some practice exercises to reinforce what you've studied.

YOUR TURN

Match the subject pronouns with the appropriate conjugations. Write the letter in the blank.

1. yo _____
2. ellos _____
3. tú _____
4. él _____
5. vosotras _____
6. nosotros _____

a. repites
b. guío
c. continúan
d. defiende
e. distribuís
f. pensamos

Use what you learned to fill in the gaps in the following verb charts.

7. pensar (to think)

Person	Singular	Plural
1st	yo _____	nosotros pensamos nosotras _____
2nd	tú _____	vosotros _____ vosotras _____
3rd	él _____ ella piensa usted piensa	ellos _____ ellas piensan ustedes _____

8. destruir (to destroy)

Person	Singular	Plural
1st	yo _____	nosotros destruimos nosotras destruimos
2nd	tú _____	vosotros _____ vosotras destruís
3rd	él _____ ella _____ usted _____	ellos _____ ellas _____ ustedes _____

7

CHAPTER 7
IRREGULAR VERBS
(PRESENT TENSE)

When I had crappy days back home, the one thing that would cheer me up was watching *Passions*. So after lunch I go into the living room and flip on the TV, expecting to find out what's going on between Sheridan and Luis, Teresa and the Crane du jour, and Charity and Miguel. Señora's napping, Ernesto's off in some other part of the house, Señor has to go back to the office, and the girls have retreated to their room. I'm all alone—and I'm happy about it. I look at the TV. The thing has to be from the '70s. What's more, it doesn't take long to realize that whatever cable package the Capelos have doesn't include any American TV stations, and without American TV stations, it's a little bit hard to watch Passions. My heart sinks. I flip through the stations aimlessly for a minute or two, not knowing what else to do, and finally give up in despair. I feel tears welling up behind my eyes as the theme music and opening credits of a Spanish program start up. The title, *Todos Los Niños*, appears on screen in Gothic letters that sort of undulate as if they were floating on water.

All the Little Children? What kind of name for a show is that? I guess it must be some sort of Spanish soap opera. When the characters appear onscreen in costumes, I realize it's the historical period show I was watching in the airport. I glaze over numbly for a while, letting the words pour over me and not making too much of an effort to figure out what's going on.

Nevertheless, after a while I start to get the characters sort of figured out. The trampy blond chambermaid, Margo, seems to be carrying on some kind of affair with the man who owns the mansion and all the land around it, Don Pedro. The beautiful brunette with the gem hanging from her neck, Doña Beatriz, seems to be estranged from her husband, and she's always acting tragic and anguished about something. Midway through the show, she's down on her knees in front of Don Pedro, imploring him for something, and he seems to be relenting toward her. But later, this gypsy tarot card reader comes in and reads Don Pedro's cards, and something she says makes him really angry, and he practically throws Doña Beatriz out of his house.

OK. So, it's not *Passions*, but it is sort of equally bad and melodramatic. It will have to do, at least until I can get back home.

IRREGULAR VERBS

You know all about regular verbs in the present tense. You've even learned which verbs experience stem changes in conjugation. You're a regular verb expert. So now let's expand your horizons a little by learning about irregular verbs in the present tense.

There are two kinds of irregular verbs in Spanish. For the sake of clarity, we'll call them regular irregulars and true irregulars. That sounds crazy, we admit it. But it will all make sense to you in a moment.

REGULAR IRREGULAR VERBS

Regular irregular verbs are pretty easy. They are only irregular in the *yo* form of present tense. Take a look at the following verb charts.

-*GO* VERBS

CAER (TO FALL)

Person	Singular	Plural
1st	yo caigo	nosotros caemos
2nd	tú caes	vosotros caéis
3rd	él cae ella cae usted cae	ellos caen ellas caen ustedes caen

See how all the other forms of the verb look the same as the regular verbs we studied in the last chapter? They follow the same rules. The only thing that is different is the *yo* form.

HACER (TO DO, TO MAKE)

Person	Singular	Plural
1st	yo hago	nosotros hacemos
2nd	tú haces	vosotros hacéis
3rd	él hace ella hace usted hace	ellos hacen ellas hacen ustedes hacen

PONER (TO PUT)

Person	Singular	Plural
1st	yo pongo	nosotros ponemos
2nd	tú pones	vosotros ponéis
3rd	él pone ella pone usted pone	ellos ponen ellas ponen ustedes ponen

Other verbs like *poner*:

componer	(to fix)
suponer	(to suppose)

SALIR (TO GO OUT)

Person	Singular	Plural
1st	yo salgo	nosotros salimos
2nd	tú sales	vosotros salís
3rd	él sale ella sale usted sale	ellos salen ellas salen ustedes salen

The following -go verbs have an irregular, first-person singular conjugation and a stem-change.

DECIR (TO SAY)

Person	Singular	Plural
1st	yo digo	nosotros decimos
2nd	tú dices	vosotros decís
3rd	él dice ella dice usted dice	ellos dicen ellas dicen ustedes dicen

TENER (TO HAVE)

Person	Singular	Plural
1st	yo tengo	nosotros tenemos
2nd	tú tienes	vosotros tenéis
3rd	él tiene ella tiene usted tiene	ellos tienen ellas tienen ustedes tienen

VENIR (TO COME)

Person	Singular	Plural
1st	yo vengo	nosotros venimos
2nd	tú vienes	vosotros venís
3rd	él viene ella viene usted viene	ellos vienen ellas vienen ustedes vienen

-*ZCO* VERBS

CONOCER (TO KNOW)

Person	Singular	Plural
1st	yo conozco	nosotros conocemos
2nd	tú conoces	vosotros conocéis
3rd	él conoce	ellos conocen
	ella conoce	ellas conocen
	usted conoce	ustedes conocen

PARECER (TO APPEAR)

Person	Singular	Plural
1st	yo parezco	nosotros parecemos
2nd	tú pareces	vosotros parecéis
3rd	él parece	ellos parecen
	ella parece	ellas parecen
	usted parece	ustedes parecen

-*OY* VERBS

DAR (TO GIVE)

Person	Singular	Plural
1st	yo doy	nosotros damos
2nd	tú das	vosotros dais
3rd	él da	ellos dan
	ella da	ellas dan
	usted da	ustedes dan

ESTAR (TO BE)

Person	Singular	Plural
1st	yo estoy	nosotros estamos
2nd	tú estás	vosotros estáis
3rd	él está ella está usted está	ellos están ellas están ustedes están

OTHER IRREGULAR VERBS

SABER (TO KNOW)

Person	Singular	Plural
1st	yo sé	nosotros sabemos
2nd	tú sabes	vosotros sabéis
3rd	él sabe ella sabe usted sabe	ellos saben ellas saben ustedes saben

VER (TO SEE)

Person	Singular	Plural
1st	yo veo	nosotros vemos
2nd	tú ves	vosotros veis
3rd	él ve ella ve usted ve	ellos ven ellas ven ustedes ven

TRUE IRREGULAR VERBS

Some verbs have irregular forms in most or all of the conjugations. Let's consider these true irregulars. Take a look at the following verbs.

HABER (TO HAVE)

Person	Singular	Plural
1st	yo he	nosotros hemos
2nd	tú has	vosotros habéis
3rd	él ha	ellos han
	ella ha	ellas han
	usted ha	ustedes han

Haber has a special, third-person singular form: *hay*. This verb means "there is" or "there are." It is not used with a subject. Take a look at the examples below. These forms of *haber* are also used in compound tenses, which you will learn about in future chapters.

Hay cinco platos en la mesa.   (There are five plates on the table.)
Hay un columpio en el parque.   (There is a swing at the park.)

IR (TO GO)

Person	Singular	Plural
1st	yo voy	nosotros vamos
2nd	tú vas	vosotros vais
3rd	él va	ellos van
	ella va	ellas van
	usted va	ustedes van

SER (TO BE)

Person	Singular	Plural
1st	yo soy	nosotros somos
2nd	tú eres	vosotros sois
3rd	él es	ellos son
	ella es	ellas son
	usted es	ustedes son

YOUR TURN

Fill in the blanks with the correct form of the verb in parentheses.

1. Yo _____ (tener) un hermano y una hermana.
2. Tú _____ (ser) muy simpático, Martín.
3. ¿Vosotros _____ (ir) al supermercado hoy?
4. Los profesores de español _____ (ir) a una conferencia.
5. Yo _____ (conocer) a la amiga de Pedro.
6. Nosotros _____ (ser) estudiantes.
7. Yo _____ (ver) un carro rojo en el garaje.
8. _____ (Haber) tres libros en mi mochila.
9. Anita _____ (tener) un perro y un gato.
10. Yo _____ (venir) a casa en autobús.

Select the right form of the verb. Write the letter in the space provided.

11. _____ una manzana en la refrigeradora.
    (A) Han (B) Hay (C) Hemos

12. ¿Tú _____ el libro de español?
    (A) tenemos (B) tengo (C) tienes

13. Vosotros _____ todas las mañanas.
    (A) salís (B) sale (C) salgo

14. Ustedes _____ al gimnasio.
    (A) voy (B) van (C) vamos

15. Yo _____ muy cansado.
    (A) estás (B) está (C) estoy

16. ¿_____ un teléfono el la casa?
    (A) Han (B) Hay (C) Hemos

CHAPTER 8
ADJECTIVES

When I get home from school the next day, Ernesto is the only one in the house.

"My mom left the dinner," he says. I stop. Did he just speak in English?

"What did you say?"

"I said my mom left the dinner."

"You speak English?!!!"

"A little," he admitted.

"I don't believe it! All this time I've been making a fool of myself trying to speak Spanish and you haven't helped a bit."

"I especially liked the part where you insulted my father."

"Oh yeah. And I suppose you knew all about the orange juice?"

"I must admit yes." He's laughing. "A little joke."

"Very funny. And it sounds like you speak more than a little English."

What a jerk. And to make it worse, after we get our plates, he comes into the living room with me to watch TV. So much for *Todos Los Niños*—he'll probably want to watch soccer or something boring like that. But just as I'm about to leave, I hear the *Los Niños* theme, and see the titles undulating across the screen. Then he actually asks me if it's OK if we watch it.

"Um, sure," I say. "You watch this show?"

"I never miss it." Wow. A guy who's into soaps. That's different.

It turns out not to be such a bad thing, because as we watch, Ernesto catches me up a bit. As I could tell from the episode I had watched, Margo, the blond chambermaid, is trying to steal Don Pedro away from Doña Beatriz so she can be the lady of the house. Plus, as I should have guessed from the crystal ball, Margo is actually a witch. What I didn't understand is that the gem Doña Beatriz wears is supposed to have magical properties that Doña Beatriz doesn't know about, so Margo's scheming to get that for herself as well. In yesterday's episode, Doña Beatriz was imploring Don Pedro to take her back, and Don Pedro's feelings for her were starting to return, but then the gypsy came and told him, while reading his cards, that he isn't really the father of his son Orlando—Orlando's father is actually Don Pedro's brother, Don John. No wonder Don Pedro is mad at Doña Beatriz!

Judging from the episode we're watching today, Don John is a very bad man. He spends most of the episode drunk, and toward the end of it he accosts Doña Beatriz, grabbing for the gem around her neck. Then the credits roll.

DESCRIPTIVE ADJECTIVES

In Chapter 3, we briefly discussed adjectives. You know what an adjective is, right? **Adjectives** modify nouns. There are all kinds of adjectives. Let's study a few of them.

A **descriptive adjective** describes a person, place, or thing. Remember the examples we gave you in Chapter 3?

la silla roja	(the red chair)
el niño bueno	(the good boy)

The adjectives *roja* and *bueno* modify the nouns *silla* and *niño*.

ADJECTIVE-NOUN AGREEMENT

You've already learned that verbs need to agree in number with their subjects. Adjectives, too, must agree with the nouns they modify. They should agree with them in both gender and number.

GENDER

If the noun is masculine, the adjective must be masculine too. If the noun is feminine, the adjective must be feminine. Usually masculine adjectives end in -*o* and a feminine adjectives end in -*a*. Take a look at these examples.

el libro viejo	(the old book)
la casa vieja	(the old house)

Some adjectives don't end in -*a* or -*o*. These adjectives can generally modify either feminine or masculine nouns.

| el hombre joven | (the young man) |
| la mujer joven | (the young woman) |

Masculine adjectives that end in -*án*, -*ón*, or -*or* can be made feminine by adding -*a*.

| un hombre hablador | (a talkative man) |
| una mujer habladora | (a talkative woman) |

NUMBER

If a noun is plural, it's accompanying adjective should be plural too. To form the plural, add -*s* to an adjective that ends with a vowel.

| los libros viejos | (the old books) |
| las casas viejas | (the old houses) |

Add -*es* to an adjective that ends with a consonant.

| los hombres jovenes | (the young man) |
| las mujeres jovenes | (the young woman) |

If an adjective ends with a -*z*, change the *z* to a *c* and add -*es*.

| el niño feliz | (the happy boy) |
| los niños felices | (the happy boys) |

As with subject pronouns, use the masculine plural ending to describe a group of masculine and female nouns.

los niñ**os** travies**os** (the naughty children)

niños/niñas *or* niños

las niñas travies**as** (the naughty girls)

niñas

SHORT AND LONG ADJECTIVES

Some descriptive adjectives have both long and short versions.

Some adjectives drop their final -o when they come before a singular, masculine noun. Take a look at these examples.

un libro   un buen libro   (a good book)

Other words like *bueno*:

alguno   (some)
malo   (bad)
primero   (first)

Grande becomes *gran* in front of any singular noun. However, the meaning changes.

un evento grande (a big event)   un gran evento (a great event)

EL GRAN ADJETIVO

Be careful with *grande* and *gran*—if you say, "*Es una grande mujer*," you're saying, "She's a great woman." However, if you say, "*Es una mujer grande*," you're saying, "She's a big woman"! You wouldn't want to say that about your Spanish teacher, especially if she's there to hear you!

Santo becomes *San* in front of any masculine name, unless the name begins with *To-* or *Do-*.

San Nicolás   San Francisco   Santo Tomás   Santo Domingo

ADJECTIVE PLACEMENT

Descriptive adjectives like *guapo* (good-looking), *hermosa* (beautiful), and *delgada* (thin) usually come after the nouns they describe.

una actor guapo   (a good-looking actor)
una actriz hermosa   (a beautiful actress)

This is obviously different from English, and it's something that you have to look out for.

Adjectives that indicate a number or quantity, however, usually go before the nouns they describe.

algunos actores guapos   (some good-looking actors)
muchas actrices hermosas   (many beautiful actresses)

Other words like *algunos* and *muchas*:

ambos	(both)
ningún	(no, not one, not any)
varios	(various)

As we explained in the previous section, some adjectives change meaning depending on where they're placed. *Gran* and *grande* are two examples. Other examples are:

un viejo amigo	(a longtime friend)
un amigo viejo	(an elderly friend)
una mujer pobre	(a woman with no money)
una pobre mujer	(a pitiful woman)

POSSESSIVE ADJECTIVES

Adjectives don't only have to be descriptive. **Possessive adjectives**, as their name suggests, indicate possession. Like all adjectives, they agree with the nouns they describe. They can be short or long.

SHORT POSSESSIVE ADJECTIVES

These are the short possessive adjectives.

For a singular noun:

Person	Singular		Plural	
1st	mi mochila/ mi libro	my backpack/ book	nuestra mochila/ nuestro libro	our backpack/ book
2nd	tu mochila/ tu libro	your backpack/ book	vuestra mochila/ vuestro libro	your backpack/ book
3rd	su mochila/ su libro	his, her, its, your (formal) backpack/book	su mochila/ su libro	their, your (formal) backpack/book

For a plural noun:

Person	Singular		Plural	
1st	mis mochilas/ mis libros	my backpacks/ books	nuestras mochilas/ nuestros libros	our backpacks/ books
2nd	tus mochilas/ tus libros	your backpacks/ books	vuestras mochilas/ vuestros libros	your backpacks/ books
3rd	sus mochilas/ sus libros	his, her, its, your (formal) backpacks/books	sus mochilas/ sus libros	their, your (formal) backpacks/ books

Short possessive adjectives always come before the nouns they modify.

Mi carro es viejo.   (My car is old.)
No tengo mis libros hoy.   (I don't have my books today.)

LONG POSSESSIVE ADJECTIVES

These are the long possessive adjectives. Long possessive adjectives always follow the noun they describe.

For a singular noun:

Person	Singular		Plural	
1st	mío/mía	of mine	nuestro/ nuestra	of ours
2nd	tuyo/tuya	of yours	vuestra/vuestro	of yours
3rd	suyo/suya	of his, hers, its, yours (formal)	suyo/suya	of theirs, yours (formal)

For a plural noun:

Person	Singular		Plural	
1st	míos/mías	of mine	nuestros/nuestras	of ours
2nd	tuyos/tuyas	of yours	vuestras/vuestros	of yours
3rd	suyos/suyas	of his, hers, its, yours (formal)	suyos/suyas	of theirs, yours (formal)

Use long possessive adjectives when you would say "of . . ." in English.

Es una amiga mía.   (She is a friend of mine.)

You can also use long possessive adjectives after the verb *ser*.

La caja es nuestra.   (The box is ours.)

DEMONSTRATIVE ADJECTIVES

Demonstrative adjectives distinguish one group of items from another group. Demonstrative adjectives are equivalent to the English words, *this*, *that*, *these*, and *those*. They also agree with the nouns they accompany.

Demonstrative adjectives change depending on the location of the object that you're talking about.

CLOSE TO THE SPEAKER

These demonstrative adjectives refer to something that is close to the speaker. Remember to use the right gender and number.

Singular	este libro	this book
	esta pluma	this pen
Plural	estos libros	these books
	estas plumas	these pens

¿Quieres esta manzana o estos limones?
(Do you want this apple or these limes?)

CLOSE TO THE LISTENER

These demonstrative adjectives refer to something that is close to the listener.

Singular	ese libro	that book
	esa pluma	that pen
Plural	esos libros	those books
	esas plumas	those pens

Esa blusa es fea, pero esos pantalones son bonitos.
(That blouse is ugly, but those trousers are nice.)

FAR FROM BOTH PEOPLE

These demonstrative adjectives refer to something that is far from both the speaker and listener.

Singular	aquel libro	that book
	aquella pluma	that pen
Plural	aquellos libros	those books
	aquellas plumas	those pens

¿Ves aquel pájaro? ¿Ves aquellos patos?
(Can you see that bird? Can you see those ducks?)

YOUR TURN

Fill in the blank with the correct form of the adjective in parentheses.

1. unas muchachas _____ (guapo)
2. un hombre _____ (joven)
3. unos libros _____ (bueno)
4. una mesa _____ (viejo)
5. un niño _____ (feliz)

Unscramble the following sentences. Pay attention to adjective placement. Some sentences may have more than one answer.

6. carro tengo un nuevo
7. grande perro ese es
8. es Marta hermosa
9. mochilas vuestras esas son
10. ¿tuyo aquel libro es?

CHAPTER 9
TRICKY VERBS

Momma said there'd be days like this, but she didn't say I'd have three of them in a row. Things have gotten worse, not better, since that first day when Profesor called on me and I froze. Since there are only fifteen of us on this trip, the class is a lot smaller than back home, so you get called on a lot more often. I try to keep up, but it's obvious who the lame student in this group is. Today we're reviewing tricky verbs, and Profesor asks me to say "The chicken is good."

"*El pollo es rico.*" The entire class erupts in laughter. I'm bewildered. Even Profesor is laughing.

"*El pollo es rico,*" I repeat.

"Olivia," Profesor says, "You just said that the chicken was rich. Rich like a lot of money."

"Oh, but I thought—" I didn't even get to finish my statement before Blair jumps in.

"With the verbs *ser* and *estar*, sometimes the meaning changes depending on whether they come before or after the adjective!" God, she just couldn't help herself.

"That's correct, Blair," Profesor says. "Excellent job." All I can do is nod as Profesor goes on about the traps with some other adjectives. Then, of course, later in the class I make the same mistake again with one of those exact adjectives because I hadn't been listening.

So it's a slow walk home for me. I'm taking my time when I hear a car pull up from behind me. It had been following me slowly, like a cat.

"Olivia!" someone calls from the car. I turn around and see Ernesto hanging out the driver's seat window. "Get in! We're going to be late for *Todos Los Niños*!"

"Ernesto?" I say, in a state of shock.

"I saw you walking. I was driving back from the market."

"Oh," I say. Still, it was nice of him to stop. I walk around to the passenger side door. As I reach for the handle, Ernesto hits the gas and moves the car up five or six feet. Hysterical laughter ensues. I wait, not moving.

"Come on, Olivia!" Ernesto yells. I glare at him and then walk back to the passenger side door. Again, just as I reach the handle he moves the car. Again, hysterical laughter.

"OK, I'm sorry," Ernesto says. "Seriously now, we're going to miss finding out whether Doña Beatriz gets away from Don John." I don't believe him for a minute. Slowly, I start walking to the car. When I've just reached the rear bumper, I quickly take a step forward, open the door to the back seat, and fall inside, just as Ernesto hits the gas again. He looks back in disbelief. Four years of basketball practice make you quicker than you look, I guess.

"Home, James," I say, and let Ernesto chauffeur me to the house.

SER AND ESTAR

Let's start with *ser* and *estar*, since they're two of the most important verbs you will learn in Spanish. If you look up *ser* and *estar* in an English-Spanish dictionary, you'll see that they both mean "to be." So which one should you use, and when? This is a very tricky part of the language to master, so take your time with these two verbs. You'll use them a lot; make sure you use the right one.

SER AS AN EQUATION

First let's go over the verb *ser*. You've already learned that it's an irregular verb. Hopefully by now you've learned how to conjugate it. Now let's learn when to use it.

Think of the verb *ser* as an equal sign (=). You remember from math that the items on either side of an equal sign must, by definition, be the same. The verb *ser* does the same thing as an equal sign. It links two elements that are grammatically similar. For example, *ser* can link two nouns, two infinitive verbs, or a pronoun and a noun. Look at the following examples.

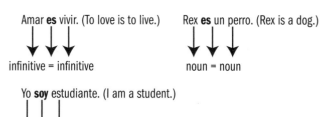

Amar **es** vivir. (To love is to live.)   Rex **es** un perro. (Rex is a dog.)

infinitive = infinitive   noun = noun

Yo **soy** estudiante. (I am a student.)

pronoun = noun

Ser can also express place of origin, when used with *de*.

Soy de Guatemala.   (I'm from Guatemala.)

SER WITH ADJECTIVES

Use *ser* to express a characteristic that is permanent or unlikely to change. For example, use *ser* with adjectives of nationality, size, or color. Look at the following examples.

Soy ecuatoriana.   (I am Ecuadorian.)
Las manzanas son rojas.   (The apples are red.)
La pelota es redonda.   (The ball is round.)

Use *ser* with adjectives that describe personal qualities too.

Miguel es alto.   (Miguel is tall)
Mi hermana es simpática.   (My sister is nice.)

Use *estar* to describe qualities that are likely to change.

Estoy cansado.   (I'm tired.)
Mauricio está nervioso.   (Mauricio is nervous.)

By using the verb *estar*, it is implied that the person in the first sentence will not always be tired, and the person in the second sentence will not always be nervous.

Think about the example *Las manzanas son rojas*. What if you were to replace *son* with *están*? *Las manzanas están rojas* implies that at one point the apples were not red or that they will not always be red. Look at the following sentences.

¡Eres bella, Margarita!
¡Estás bella, Margarita!

Can you tell what the difference is? *¡Eres bella, Margarita!* means "You're beautiful, Margarita!" *¡Estás bella, Margarita!* on the other hand, means "You look beautiful, Margarita" or "You're beautiful (right now), Margarita."

What about another example, *Miguel es alto*? If you said, *Miguel está alto*, you would be implying that he has changed height since the last time you saw him. Perhaps he was a little boy who grew up, or perhaps he works at a circus and wears stilts. Both of these possibilities are pretty remote, so consider that when you're deciding which verb is appropriate.

CHANGES IN MEANING

Some adjectives may change meaning depending on which verb is used: *ser* or *estar*. Take a look at these examples. Can you see what the difference is?

- *aburrido* ("boring" versus "bored"):

Esa película es aburrida.	(That movie is boring.)
El público está aburrido.	(The audience is bored.)

- *bueno* ("good" versus "tasty"):

La fruta es buena para la salud.	(Fruit is good for your health.)
La fruta está buena.	(Fruit is tasty.)

- *cómodo* (a "comfortable" object versus a "comfortable" person):

La silla es cómoda.	(The chair is comfortable.)
Estoy cómodo.	(I'm comfortable.)

- *rico* ("rich" versus "tasty"):

Mi tío es rico.	(My uncle is rich.)
El pollo está rico.	(The chicken is good.)

SABER AND CONOCER

The verbs *saber* and *conocer* are similar to *ser* and *estar*. *Saber* and *conocer* both translate as "to know." However, they change meaning depending on context.

Conocer means "to know someone" or "to be familiar with something."

Conozco a Luis.	(I know Luis.)
No conozco la ciudad.	(I'm not familiar with that city.)

Saber means "to know something" or, when used with the infinitive, "to know how to do something."

¿Sabes mi dirección?	(Do you know my address?)
Sé hablar español.	(I know how to speak Spanish.)

TOMAR AND LLEVAR

Tomar and *llevar* both translate as "to take." Which one should you use?

Tomar means "to take something" or "to drink something."

Tomo el autobús.	(I take the bus.)
Tomamos la llave.	(We take the key.)
¿Tomas jugo?	(Do you drink juice?)

Llevar means "to take someone or something away."

Llevo mi libro a la escuela.	(I take my book to school.)
Llevamos mis padres al concierto.	(We take my parents to the concert.)

HABER AND TENER

Haber and *tener* both translate as "to have."

As we learned in Chapter 7, the verb *haber* is mostly used as *hay*. *Hay* is equivalent to the English "there is" or "there are." It does not have a subject.

Hay un libro en la mesa.	(There is a book on the table.)
Hay tres estudiantes en el aula.	(There are three students in the classroom.)

Hay does not change to plural. Later you will see that *haber* is also used as a helping verb to express "to have."

He estudiado.	(I have studied.)

Tener means "to have something" or "to possess."

Tengo una bicicleta.	(I have a bicycle.)
Tienen dos hermanas.	(They have two sisters.)

Tener is also used in idiomatic expressions. Look at the following examples.

Tengo trece años.	(I'm thirteen years old.)
Tengo frío.	(I'm cold.)
Tengo hambre.	(I'm hungry.)
Tengo ganas de comer.	(I feel like eating.)

The verbs discussed in this chapter are both tricky and used often in everyday conversation. You must study them again and again. Even longtime students of Spanish still confuse these verbs. See where you stand by trying the following exercises.

YOUR TURN

Write the correct verb from the parentheses in the blank.

1. _____ (Soy/Estoy) tu amiga.
2. _____ (Es/Está) alto y guapo.
3. _____ (Estáis/Sois) cansados.
4. _____ (Eres/Estás) estudiante.
5. _____ (Son/Están) americanas.
6. _____ Manú (es/está) mi gato.
7. _____ (Somos/Estamos) de Argentina.
8. _____ (Están/Son) cansados.
9. _____ Cantar (es/estar) vivir.
10. _____ ¿(Estás/Eres) aburrido?

Translate the following sentences into Spanish.

11. My boss (*jefe*) is rich.
12. Katie is nine years old.
13. We drink milk (*leche*).
14. The boys know how to speak German (*alemán*).
15. There are two apples in the refrigerator (*refrigeradora*).
16. Do you take the bus to school?

10

CHAPTER 10
ADVERBS

The Capelos residence only has one bathroom. Señor and Señora get up way earlier than everyone else, so they are in the clear, but Emilia and Cristina, my two sisters, and I all have to use the bathroom within the space of an hour or so. Señora came up with this schedule for us to avoid confusion in the morning, especially as some of us have a tendency to be not so nice when we don't have our orange juice. Emilia goes first, at 7:15. I go second, at 7:30, and Cristina goes last, at 7:45, mainly because she moves so *lentamente*.[1] I totally expedite my own bathroom routine for the sake of *la familia* and move most of my beauty regimen to my room so others can use the bathroom. I'm quite proud of myself, actually.

However, this morning, when I head for the shower at my appointed time, the door is still closed. Strange. I go to Emilia's room and see that she's already there.

"*¿Quién está en el baño?*"[2] I ask.

"*Oh, creo que Ernesto.*"[3] Ernesto? What? That doesn't make any sense. He usually doesn't get up until noon. I go back and stand by the bathroom door. This is incredible. Who does this guy think he is? I have to leave in like half an hour and I can't even get into the bathroom. He's screwing up the schedule.

"What a selfish pig," I think. "He didn't even ask." I somehow doubt it's even Ernesto at all. Maybe it's Cristina. Soon, though, I hear singing. Yes, it's unmistakably Ernesto. It's also unmistakably Madonna, though it takes me a moment to put the words together given his accent.

"Don't go for second best, baby, put your lover to the test, you know you know you know you got to make him express how he feels and baby then you know your love is real. Express himself. Yay yay yay yay."

---

1   slowly
2   Who is in the bathroom?
3   Oh, I think it's Ernesto.

I can't help but laugh, even though I won't be able to take a shower before school. Madonna. Who knew?

ADVERBS

In Chapter 3, we explained that an **adverb** modifies a verb, adjective, or other adverb. Here are some examples of adverbs.

Antonietta habla **bien**. (Antonietta speaks well.)

Caminas **lentamente**. (You walk slowly.)

As you can see, in Spanish the adverb is placed close to the word it modifies.

-MENTE ADVERBS

The easiest adverbs are those that end in -*mente*. Think of -*mente* as -*ly*. Easy, right? This is how you form them: Add -*mente* to the feminine form of the adjective.

Adjective	Feminine + -*mente*
lento	lentamente (slowly)

Remember that some adjectives don't have a feminine form. In this case, take the base form of the adjective, and then add -*mente*.

Adjective	Adjective + -*mente*
alegre	alegremente (happily)

When you put together a string of -*mente* adverbs, drop the ending for all but the last one. Take a look at this example.

La profesora habla clara y lentamente. (The teacher speaks clearly and slowly.)

ADVERBS THAT ANSWER QUESTIONS

Other adverbs are not as easy to remember, because they don't follow the -*mente* pattern. You'll have to memorize these. However, this will be easier if you think of them as answering the questions ¿*cómo*?, ¿*dónde*?, ¿*cuándo*?, and ¿*cuánto*?

MANNER

¿Cómo? adverbs answer the question "how?" These adverbs are also called **adverbs of manner**.

¿Cómo cocinas?	(How do you cook?)
Cocino bien.	(I cook well.)

Other adverbs like *bien*:

Adverbs of Manner			
así	like that	**mal**	badly
claramente	clearly	**menos**	less
de pronto	suddenly	**más**	more

PLACE

¿Dónde? adverbs answer the question "where?" These adverbs are also called **adverbs of place**.

¿Dónde está la escuela?	(Where is the school?)
La escuela está cerca.	(The school is close.)

Other adverbs like *cerca*:

Adverbs of Place			
abajo	below	**arriba**	above
acá	over here	**debajo**	underneath
adelante	in front	**delante**	in front
adentro	inside	**detrás**	behind
aquí	here	**encima**	on top
allá	over there	**lejos**	far

TIME

¿Cuándo? adverbs answer the question "when?" These adverbs are also called **adverbs of time**.

¿Cuándo vas al aeropuerto?	(When are you going to the airport?)
Voy pronto al aeropuerto.	(I'm going to the airport soon.)

Other adverbs like *pronto*:

Adverbs of Time			
Time of Day			
ahora	now	**mañana**	tomorrow
hoy	today	**de día**	during the day
anoche	last night	**de noche**	at night
ayer	yesterday	**a la una** (a las dos, etc.)	at one o'clock (at two, etc.)
Relative Time			
a veces	sometimes	**nunca**	never
antes	before	**siempre**	always
después	after	**tarde**	late
entonces	then	**temprano**	early
luego	later	**todavía**	still
mientras	during	**ya**	already

QUANTITY

¿Cuánto? adverbs answer the question "how much?" These adverbs are also called **adverbs of quantity**.

¿Cuánto habla Patricia?	(How much does Patricia talk?)
¡Patricia habla demasiado!	(Patricia talks too much!)

Other adverbs like *demasiado*:

Adverbs of Quantity			
algo	a bit, rather	**menos**	less
apenas	barely	**mucho**	a lot
bastante	a lot	**muy**	very
casi	almost	**nada**	not at all
cuanto	as much	**poco**	a little
más	more	**sólo**	only
medio	half	**tanto**	so much

CONFIRMATION, NEGATION, AND DOUBT

Adverbs can also be used to confirm, negate, and express doubt. These are called **adverbs of confirmation**, **adverbs of negation**, and **adverbs of doubt**.

Take a look at the following chart.

Adverbs of Confirmation			
claro	of course	**por supuesto**	of course
sí	yes	**ya**	all right
sin duda	without a doubt		
Adverbs of Negation			
no	no	**claro que no**	of course not
tampoco	neither		
Adverbs of Doubt			
acaso	perhaps, maybe	**quisás**	maybe
tal vez	maybe		

MULTIPLE FUNCTION WORDS

Some words can be adverbs or adjectives, depending on their function in the sentence.

Comen **mucho** pan. (They eat a lot of bread.)   Corren **mucho**. (They run a lot.)

In the first sentence, *mucho* modifies *pan* and is an adjective. In the second sentence, *mucho* modifies *corren* and is an adverb. There is one important difference between adjectives and adverbs: Adjectives change according to the nouns they modify, but adverbs don't.

Comen **muchos** panes. (They eat a lot of bread.)

Other words like *mucho*:

poco	(a little)
bastante	(a lot)
algo	(some)
nada	(none)

That's it for adverbs! See if you've learned a lot by trying out the exercises.

YOUR TURN

Turn the following adjectives into adverbs.

1. final
2. nervioso
3. claro
4. raro
5. breve

Fill in the blank with the correct adverb. Use each word only once.

tanto   por supesto   un poco   también   acá   mucho   algo
luego   siempre   muy

6. Estoy _____ (*rather*) cansada hoy.
7. El niño corre _____ (*very*) rápidamente.
8. _____ (*of course*) que voy a la escuela hoy.
9. Quiero _____ (*a little*) de sopa, por favor.
10. Tu mochila está _____ (*here*).
11. Vamos _____ (*later*) al supermercado.
12. ¡El bebé llora (*cries*) _____ (*so much*)!
13. Quiero ese jugo _____ (*also*).
14. Mi madre está _____ (*always*) ocupada (*busy*).
15. Me gustan (*I like*) _____ (*a lot*) las manzanas verdes.

11

CHAPTER 11
NEGATIVE STATEMENTS

My first Saturday in Costa Rica. Strangely, I get up at the usual time. Back home I usually sleep late on the weekends, but here I'm up before I know it. I walk out into the kitchen and Señor and Señora are at their usual spots at the kitchen table.

"*Buenos días,* Olivia," Señor says. Señora gets up from the table and gets me a glass of orange juice. She gives me a knowing smile.

"*Gracias,*" I say and take a seat next to Señor.

"*Bueno,* Olivia," Señor says. "*Es tu primer fin de semana en Costa Rica. ¿Qué haces?*"[1]

"Oh, *no sé,*[2] I say, which is the truth. I have no idea.

"*Pues, ¿su grupo no tiene una actividad o algo?*"[3]

"*No, este fin de semana, no.*"[4] Señor and Señora exchange glances, and I drink my orange juice. Ernesto walks in.

"*Buenos,*"[5] he says to everyone, then sits down. Señora gets up and brings him a glass and the pitcher of orange juice. "*Y Olivia, ¿que haces hoy?* It's your first weekend in Costa Rica!"

"I know, your dad just asked me that as well," I say. "I have no idea."

"*¿Comó? ¿Ninguna idea? Entonces vamos a la cuidad.*[6] We'll go into the city together. I'll show you the sights."

Well, I think, I certainly have nothing better to do. Why not?

We take the bus downtown, zig-zagging through traffic. The bus drivers here are maniacs; they assume that because they're so much bigger than the tiny compact cars most people in San José drive, everybody else will get out of the

---

1 Olivia, it is your first weekend in Costa Rica. What are you doing?
2 Oh, I don't know.
3 Well, your group does not have an activity or something?
4 Not this weekend.
5 Good morning! (*Buenos* is short for *buenos días.*)
6 What? No idea? Then let's go into the city!

way. And, actually, most of the time it works. However, it doesn't make for the most pleasant ride.

The bus drops us off at the Museo Nacional first. It's in this old building that used to be a fort right in the middle of the city.

"This is our Museo Nacional," Ernesto says, looking at me out of the corner of his eye.

"Very nice," I say.

"Yes. The *museo* is an old fort." I nod.

"Do you want to go in?" he asks cautiously.

"Um, well, do you want to?" There are few things I have less desire to do than spend a beautiful sunny day in a stuffy old museum. Even if it did use to be an old fort.

"Me? I have been many, many times."

"Well, then I don't really see the need—"

"Ah, excellent," Ernesto says with a laugh and a sigh. "I really didn't want to go. Let's go shopping instead!"

"Wow, it's so strange to hear a guy say that."

"Why?"

"Because in the United States guys aren't supposed to like shopping. It's sort of a girly thing to do."

"Really? I love shopping. My friends and I go all the time. Do you think I'm girly now?"

"Not at all," I say, putting my hand through his arm.

NEGATIVE STATEMENTS

The easiest way to say *no* in Spanish is to simply say *no*. No problem, right? Just like in English.

¿Quieres tu abrigo?	(Do you want your coat?)
No.	(No.)

If you'd like to be a little more polite, add *gracias*.

¿Quieres tu abrigo?	(Do you want your coat?)
No, gracias. Hace calor.	(No, thank you. It's warm out.)

You learned in Chapter 10 that adverbs of negation can be used to negate actions. The word *no* always precedes the verb it negates. Take a look at these examples.

Sara **no** tiene computadora. (Sara does not have a computer.)

No puedo comer. (I can't eat.)

NEGATIVE AND AFFIRMATIVE WORDS

Here are other negative words. Take a look at the affirmative words with which they correspond. This will help you understand them better.

Negative		Affirmative	
nada	nothing, not anything	**algo**	something
nadie	no one, not anyone, nobody	**alguien**	someone, anyone
nadie	nobody, no one, not anything	**cualquiera**	anybody, any
ninguno, ninguna	no, no one, none, neither	**alguno**, **alguna**	some, someone, any
ninguno	nobody, no one, none, not any	**algunos, algunas, unos**	some, several, any
nunca, jamás	never	**alguna vez**	ever
		siempre	always
tampoco	either, not neither	**también**	also, too

Remember: *Ninguno/a* is only used in the singular form.

USING NEGATIVE AND AFFIRMATIVE WORDS

Affirmative words are generally easy to use. Negative words, however, are a little trickier. You'll notice that double (and multiple) negatives are common in Spanish—in fact, sometimes you *must* use a double negative. The rules are easy: If *no* or another negative word proceeds the verb, all words that follow must be negative.

No quiero nada.	(I don't want anything.)
No canta ninguno de mis hermanos.	(None of my siblings sing.)

If a negative word comes after the verb in a sentence with another negative word, don't use the word *no*.

Nunca como espinaca.	(I never eat spinach.)

Here are some more rules to follow when using negative and affirmative words.

ALGUIEN AND NADIE

Alguien and *nadie* refer to people and are always in the singular. When *alguien* and *nadie* are the direct object of a verb, you must use the word *a* before it. To identify the direct object of a verb, ask yourself: Who or what is receiving the direct action of the verb?

verb   direct object
<u>¿Conoces a alguien</u> aquí?   (Do you know anyone here?)

verb   direct object
No <u>conozco a nadie</u> aquí.   (I don't know anyone here.)

When *alguien* or *nadie* is the subject of the sentence, it does not require *a*.

Alguien te llama.	(Someone is calling you.)
Nadie está en casa.	(No one's home.)

ALGUNO AND NINGUNO

Alguno and *ninguno* refer to objects or people. When *alguno* and *ninguno* come in front of a masculine, singular noun, they get shortened to *algún* and *ningún*.

¿Hay algún libro aquí?	(Are there any books here?)
No hay ningún libro aquí.	(There are no books here.)

Use the word *a* when *alguno* or *ninguno* is the direct object of a verb and refers to a person.

verb   direct object
¿<u>Conoces</u> <u>a algún profesor</u>?   (Do you know any teachers?)

verb   direct object
No <u>conozco</u> <u>a ningún profesor</u>.   (I don't know any teachers.)

verb   direct object
<u>Veo</u> <u>a algunos niños</u> en el parque.   (I see some kids at the park.)

As you can see from the above example, *alguno* can be plural (*algunos*). So can *ninguno* (*ningunos*).

TAMBIÉN AND TAMPOCO

También expresses agreement with an affirmative statement.

Yo quiero ir.   (I want to go.)
Yo quiero ir también.   (I want to go too.)

Tampoco expresses agreement with a negative statement.

Yo no quiero ir.   (I don't want to go.)
Yo no quiero ir tampoco.   (I don't want to go either.)

In the second example, the word *no* forces us to use the negative *tampoco*. We are not allowed to use double negatives in English, so in this case, *tampoco* is translated as "not either."

PERO AND SINO

Pero and *sino* often accompany negative and affirmative words. Both mean "but." However, they are used differently.

Pero means "but nevertheless."

No soy norteamericano pero hablo inglés.
(I'm not American, but nevertheless, I speak English.)

Sino, on the other hand, means "but rather."

Los libros no son viejos sino nuevos.   (The books are not old, but rather new.)

NEGATIVE AND AFFIRMATIVE EXPRESSIONS

Here are some key expressions with negative and affirmative words.

Negative Expressions		Affirmative Expressions	
en ninguna parte	nowhere	**en alguna parte**	somewhere
de ninguna manera	in no way	**de alguna manera**	somehow
ni siquiera	not even	**alguna vez**	ever
ya no	no longer	**algunas veces**	sometimes
todavía no	not yet		

El lápiz tiene que estar en alguna parte. (The pencil has to be somewhere.)
Ya no sé hablar inglés. (I don't know how to speak English anymore.)

Now you should be able to know when—and when not—to use negative words. Try these practice exercises before you move on to Chapter 12.

YOUR TURN

Rewrite the following affirmative sentences as negative sentences. There may be more than one answer. Remember the rules for double negatives.

1. Algunos de mis amigos viven allí.
2. Necesitamos algo. (*necesitar = to need*)
3. Siempre estudio con alguien.
4. ¿Queréis ir a la fiesta (*party*)?
5. Hay algo en la refrigeradora.
6. Siempre coméis desayuno (*breakfast*).
7. Conozco a algún niño americano.
8. Siempre voy al gimnasio (*gym*).
9. Los alumnos tienen una computadora.
10. Amo a alguien. (*amar = to love*)

Fill in the blank with the appropriate word: *también*, *tampoco*, *sino*, or *pero*.

11. Victoria no quiere café, y yo _____
12. No soy fea (*ugly*), _____ bonita (*pretty*).
13. Ellos necesitan un suéter. Ellas _____ necesitan un suéter.
14. Juan Pablo no come carne, _____ sí come pescado (*fish*).
15. Soy ecuatoriana. Marta _____ es ecuatoriana.
16. El profesor no es bueno, _____malo.
17. La televisión es vieja _____ todavía funciona. (*funcionar = to work or to function properly*)
18. El gato no es vegetariano. El perro _____ es vegetariano.
19. Mi abuelo (*grandfather*) toma medicina. Mi abuela _____ toma medicina.
20. El programa no es interesante, _____ aburrido (*boring*).

12

CHAPTER 12
DIRECT AND INDIRECT OBJECT PRONOUNS

Yesterday was by far the best day in Costa Rica yet. Ernesto and I spent the whole day downtown. We went into some cool stores, had coffee at an outdoor café, and talked about soap operas, which, by the way, are called *telenovelas* here. It was a little weird at first, because I've never done these things with a guy before. But Ernesto's actually really funny when he talks about them—he even does this great imitation of Doña Beatriz acting all sobby and tragic. Doña B. is by far our favorite character, and Ernesto agrees with me that that blond bimbo chambermaid, Margo, has got to go.

Ernesto also told me all about his favorite show of the year: the annual Latin American soap opera awards show.

"It's so much fun to see the actors out of their roles and all glammed up," he says, as we sit outside in the sun with our coffee. "Some of them are just in ten thousand-dollar gowns, but some of them go totally overboard with feathers, huge hats, and stuff like that. Last year Elivira, who plays Doña B, wore a bridal gown! You should have seen it. The whole show is like the Oscars, but way more over the top. The awards are in San José again this year."

"Really?" I said.

"Yes, and since you are now a *Todos Los Niños* fan, you have to watch with me. The best part is before the show starts, with the . . . the . . . *¿alfombra roja? ¿Me comprendes?*"

"The red carpet?"

"*Exactamente.* Yes, that. The red carpet. To watch them walk in."

"They have that here too?"

"Of course. It's so much fun! I went four years ago, the last time they were here in San José."

DIRECT AND INDIRECT OBJECT PRONOUNS

Before we go over direct and indirect object pronouns, let's review direct and indirect objects. We touched on direct objects in Chapter 11, but it's time to go over them more in depth. You'll need to understand what they are before we delve into the pronouns.

REVIEW: DIRECT OBJECTS

What is a direct object? The **direct object** of a sentence is who or what is receiving the direct action of the verb. Take a look at the following sentences.

subject   verb   direct object
The <u>woman</u> <u>feeds</u> the <u>baby</u> .

To identify the direct object of the sentence, turn the sentence into a question. Ask yourself, Whom does the woman feed? The answer—the baby—is the direct object.

subject   verb   direct object
<u>María Clara</u> <u>eats</u> <u>cereal</u>.

What does María Clara eat? Cereal.

Can you identify the direct objects of this sentence?

El profesor enseña inglés.   (The professor teaches English.)

If you said *inglés*, you're right. To identify the direct object of this sentence, ask yourself, What does the *profesor* teach? English. Thus, English is the direct object.

REVIEW: THE PERSONAL *A*

Direct objects work the same in Spanish as they do in English. However, there is one little rule to remember: In Spanish, when the direct object of a verb is a person, it must be preceded by an *a*. You've actually seen this *a* before, in Chapter 11 (when we discussed *alguien*, *nadie*, *alguno*, and *ninguno*). If you recall, when any of these words are a direct object and refer to people, they are accompanied by *a*. This *a* is called the **personal *a***. The personal *a* signals that the person that follows is a direct object and will receive the direct action of the verb.

Take a look at these sentences.

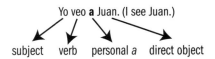

Yo veo **a** Juan. (I see Juan.)

subject   verb   personal *a*   direct object

The personal *a* is necessary because Juan is a person.

In the following sentence, the personal *a* is not necessary. Do you know why?

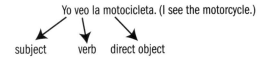

Yo veo la motocicleta. (I see the motorcycle.)

subject   verb   direct object

The personal *a* is not necessary because the direct object is an object, not a person. Another rule of thumb: Always remember to contract the personal *a* and the definite article *el* to form *al*.

Invito al esposo de mi vecina.   (I invite my neighbor's husband.)

INDIRECT OBJECTS

Now that direct objects and the personal *a* are out of the way, we can learn about indirect objects. The **indirect object** of a sentence is who or what benefits, or is harmed by, the action of the verb.

Take a look at the following sentences.

ssubject   verb   indirect object
The boy gives a book to his sister.

We identify the indirect object of the sentence in the same way we identify the direct object—by turning the sentence into a question. Who does the boy give the book to? The answer—his sister—is the indirect object.

subject   verb   indirect object
The woman puts pepper on her steak.

To identify the indirect object of the sentence, ask yourself, What does the woman put pepper on? The answer? On her steak.

When you're trying to identify the indirect object of a sentence in Spanish, always look for the prepositions *a* or *para*. Be careful not to confuse the preposition *a* with the personal *a*. They serve different functions.

When *para* precedes the indirect object, the construction is simple.

indirect object

Compro una mesa para <u>la cocina</u>.   (I buy a table for the kitchen.)

When *a* precedes the indirect object, the construction is a little trickier. You have to include *le* or *les* in the sentence. These are indirect object pronouns. We'll learn more about them later on in the chapter.

indirect object

Le doy una muñeca a mi <u>hermana</u>.   (I give a doll to my sister.)

Now we're ready to learn about direct and indirect object pronouns. These are some of the hardest pronouns to master, so make sure you review these rules carefully. If you're still confused after you're done with the chapter, don't fret: Keep on practicing, and eventually they'll become easier and easier.

DIRECT OBJECT PRONOUNS

Pronouns, as you already know, replace nouns. **Direct object pronouns** replace direct object nouns.

Here are the direct obect pronouns.

For the singular:

Person		
1st	me	me
2nd	te	you
3rd	lo	him, it (masculine), you (formal)
	la	her, it (feminine), you (formal)

For the plural:

Person		
1st	nos	us
2nd	os	you
3rd	los	them (masculine), you (formal)
	las	them (feminine), you (formal)

Examples:

Mauricio ve a **Federico**. Mauricio **lo** ve. (Mauricio sees Federico. Mauricio sees him.)

Compro la **manzana**. **La** compro. (I buy the apple. I buy it.)

Te veo.	(I see you.)
José la ve.	(José sees her.)
Los conozco bién.	(I know them well.)
Os entiendo.	(I understand you.)

In affirmative sentences, the direct object pronoun comes before the verb. In negative sentences, the direct object pronoun comes between the verb and *no*.

Maribel tiene la llave. Maribel la tiene.
(Maribel has the key. Maribel has it.)

Maribel no tiene la llave. Maribel no la tiene.
(Maribel doesn't have the key. She doesn't have it.)

INDIRECT OBJECT PRONOUNS

Indirect object pronouns replace indirect object nouns.

Here are the indirect object pronouns.

For the singular:

Person		
1st	me	to/for me
2nd	te	to/for you
3rd	le	to/for him, her, it, you (formal)

For the plural:

Person		
1st	nos	to/for us
2nd	os	to/for you
3rd	les	to/for them, you (formal)

Here are some examples:

Yo **le** escribo una carta a **Susana.** (I write a letter to Susana.)

Tú **les** prestas dinero a **Martín y Ramiro**. (You lend money to Martín and Ramiro.)

If the indirect object noun is known, you can drop the indirect object noun. In this case, use only the indirect object pronoun. The preposition *a* is used when the indirect object is not understood.

Yo le escribo una carta.	(I write her a letter. *her* = Susana)
Tú les prestas dinero.	(You lend them money. *them* = Martín and Ramiro)

DOUBLE OBJECT PRONOUNS

Sometimes a verb has both a direct object pronoun and an indirect object pronoun. When this happens, the indirect object pronoun will always precede the direct object pronoun.

Escribo una carta y **te la** mando. (I write a letter and I send it to you.)

indirect object pronoun   direct object pronoun

The pronouns can go either before or after the verb. In the example above, the indirect object pronoun (*te*) appears after the verb (*escribo*). The direct object pronoun (*la*) appears before the verb (*mando*).

In some cases, both pronouns will go after the verb. They are attached to the verb. Don't forget to add an accent mark.

Quiero comprártelo.   (I want to buy it for you.)

Le and *les* change to *se* when followed by *lo, la, los,* or *las.*

Le vendo la mochila.	(I sell him/her the backpack.)
Se lo vendo.	(I sell it to him/her.)
Les compro los lápices.	(I buy them the pencils.)
Se los compro.	(I buy them for them.)

YOUR TURN

Identify the direct and indirect objects. Circle the direct objects and underline the indirect objects.

1. Compro un sombrero (*hat*) para mi amigo.
2. Enseñamos la tarea (*homework*) a la profesora. (*enseñar* = *to show*)
3. Doy la comida al perro.
4. El señor vende el suéter a la señora.
5. La mamá prepara la sopa (*soup*) para el niño.

Change the direct object noun to a direct object pronoun. Make any other necessary changes.

6. Francisco tiene el pasaporte.
7. ¿Véis a Juan?
8. Leemos la lección.
9. El muchacho escribe el párrafo (*paragraph*).
10. Yo veo la película (*movie*).

Use the cues in parentheses to provide the indirect object pronoun for the sentence. Write the pronoun in the space provided.

11. Juan _____ escribe una carta. (*to Elena and Felipe*)
12. Maite _____ canta en español. (*to us*)
13. La profesora _____ enseña los verbos. (*to me*)
14. Nosotras _____ compramos un suéter. (*for her*)
15. Yo _____ doy una manzana. (*to you, informal*)

Rewrite the following sentences. Change the underlined noun to a pronoun.

16. Te mando <u>unos regalos</u> (*gifts*).
17. Le presto <u>mi pluma</u>.
18. Le enseño <u>la camisa (*shirt*) nueva</u>.
19. Nos compra <u>una bicicleta</u>.
20. ¿Me traes <u>la bebida</u> (*drink*)? (*traer* = *to bring*)

13

CHAPTER 13
COMPARATIVES AND SUPERLATIVES

The following Monday Profesor is writing something about comparatives and superlatives on the chalkboard, but to tell you the truth I'm not really following much of it. My mind's still wandering back to my terrific Saturday with Ernesto, wondering when we'll get to go back downtown again. I guess Profesor can sort of see I'm not paying attention, because he picks on me immediately.

"*Bueno*, Olivia, *en español*, please give the class an example of how you compare two unequal things."

I feel that unpleasant rush of adrenaline as everyone turns to stare at me. I can hear Blair, under her breath, mutter, "This ought to be good."

"Um, well, *por ejemplo,*"[1] I stammer.

Profesor and the class look at me expectantly.

"*Doña Beatriz tiene más dignidad y personalidad que Margo, la bruja.*"[2] The class is silent. The Profesor finally breaks a smile.

"*Muy bien,* Olivia. *Te gustan las telenovelas, ¿no? A mi también.*"[3]

I'm in such a good mood after class that I decide to bury the hatchet and invite Blair back to lunch, something Señora has often told me I should feel free to do. Blair accepts, somewhat hesitantly.

Outside, Ernesto is sitting in his car waiting for me. He does a double-take when he sees me with Blair. Or rather, when he sees Blair with her blond locks cascading down over her shoulders.

"Oh, how cute! Chauffer service," Blair squeals.

For a moment I worry that Ernesto will pull one of his practical jokes, like rolling the car forward as we're about to get in. But instead he hops out and holds

---

1 for example
2 Doña Beatriz has more dignity and personality than Margo, the witch.
3 Very good. You like soap operas? Me too.

open the door for Blair. I get in on the other side, rolling my eyes.

"Where to, *señoritas?*" he asks, flashing his perfect white smile in Blair's direction.

Sheesh. What is it with guys and blondes?

COMPARISONS

Both Spanish and English use comparisons to compare people or things with one another. There are three kinds of comparisons: **equal than**, **greater than**, and **less than**.

COMPARISONS OF EQUALITY

When you are comparing two or more items that are equal, use the following constructions.

With adjectives and adverbs:

·   *tan* + adjective + *como*

adjective
La comida es tan <u>buena</u> como en casa.
(The food is as good as it is at home.)

·   *tan* + adverb + *como*

adverb
María habla tan <u>bien</u> como tú.
(María speaks as well as you do.)

With nouns:

·   *tanto* + masculine singular noun + *como*

masc. sing. noun
Alfredo tiene tanto <u>dinero</u> como Francisco.
(Alfredo has as much money as Francisco.)

·   *tanta* + feminine singular noun + *como*

fem. sing. noun
Tú comes tanta <u>comida</u> como mi padre.
(You eat as much food as my father does.)

·   *tantos* + masculine plural noun + *como*

masc. pl. noun

Ustedes prueban tantos platos como nosotros.
(You try as many dishes as we do.)

- *tantas* + feminine plural noun + *como*

fem. pl. noun

Yo tengo tantas amigas como mi hermana.
(I have as many friends as my sister does.)

With verbs:

- verb + *tanto como*

verb

Yo duermo tanto como mi tía.
(I sleep as much as my aunt.)

COMPARISONS OF INEQUALITY

When you are comparing two or more items and one is greater than the other, use the following constructions.

With adjectives and adverbs:

- *más* + adjective + *que*

adjective

El elefante es más grande que el caballo.
(The elephant is bigger than the horse.)

- *más* + adverb + *que*

adverb

Me acuesto más tarde que tú.
(I go to bed later than you do.)

With nouns:

- *más* + noun + *que*

noun

Magdalena tiene más discos compactos que Zoila.
(Magdalena has more compact discs than Zoila does.)

With verbs:

- verb + *más que*

  _{verb}
  Mi abuelo <u>duerme</u> más que mi abuela.
  (My grandfather sleeps more than my grandmother does.)

When you are comparing two or more items and one is less than the other, use the following constructions.

With adjectives and adverbs:

- *menos* + adjective + *que*

  _{adjective}
  La biología es menos <u>interesante</u> que la química.
  (Biology is less interesting than chemistry.)

- *menos* + adverb + *que*

  _{adverb}
  Mi hermano corre menos <u>rápido</u> que Alfredo.
  (My brother runs less quickly than Alfredo does.)

With nouns:

- *menos* + noun + *que*

  _{noun}
  Yo compro menos <u>camisas</u> que Felipe.
  (I buy fewer shirts than Felipe does.)

With verbs:

- verb + *menos que*

  _{verb}
  El bebé de Marta <u>llora</u> menos que el bebé de Adelia.
  (Marta's baby cries less than Adelia's baby does.)

IRREGULAR COMPARISON FORMS

Some adjectives and adverbs have irregular comparison forms. Do not use *más* and *menos* with these words. Take a look at the following charts.

ADJECTIVE		COMPARATIVE	
bueno/a	good	**mejor**	better
malo/a	bad	**peor**	worse
grande	big	**mayor**	bigger
pequeño/a	small	**menor**	smaller
joven	young	**menor**	younger
viejo/a	old	**mayor**	older

El café es bueno. El café es mejor que el té.
(Coffee is good. Coffee is better than tea.)

ADVERB		COMPARATIVE	
bien	well	**mejor**	better
mal	badly	**peor**	worse
mucho	a lot	**más**	more
poco	a little	**menos**	less

Gonzalo toca bien el clarinete. Toca el clarinete mejor que Ernesto.
(Gonzalo plays the clarinet well. He plays the clarinet
better than Ernesto does.)

SUPERLATIVES

Use the following constructions to express the superlative in Spanish. The noun is always preceded by a definite article, and *de* is equivalent to the English *in* or *of*.

· definite article + noun + *más* + adjective + *de*

Iris es la más guapa de mis amigas.
(Iris is the best-looking of my friends./Iris is my best-looking friend.)

· definite article + noun + *menos* + adjective + *de*

Patricio es el menos estudioso de la clase.
(Patricio is the least studious of the class.)

IRREGULAR SUPERLATIVES

As with comparatives, there are also irregular superlatives. Take a look at the following chart.

ADJECTIVE		SUPERLATIVE	
bueno/a	good	el mejor	best
malo/a	bad	el peor	worst
grande	big	el mayor	biggest
pequeño/a	small	el menor	smallest
joven	young	el menor	youngest
viejo/a	old	el mayor	oldest

When you use the superlative, make sure your definite article agrees in gender with the noun it accompanies.

Isabel es la mayor de su familia. (Isabel is the oldest in her family.)
Yo soy el mejor de la clase. (I'm the best in the class.)

ABSOLUTE SUPERLATIVES

If you want to express an even higher degree of quality, you can use the absolute superlative. In Spanish, the absolute superlative is equivalent to *extremely*, *exceptionally*, or *very* in English. This is how you form it.

For adjectives and adverbs that end in a vowel, drop the final vowel and add -*ísimo/a*.

malo   mal-   malísimo/a

¡El libro es malísimo!   (The book is very bad!)

For adjectives and adverbs that end in -c, -g, or -z, make the following spelling changes to the absolute superlative.

c	→	qu	+	-ísimo/a
		rico	→	riquísimo
g	→	gu	+	-ísimo/a
		largo	→	larguísimo
z	→	c	+	-ísimo/a
		feliz	→	felicísimo

For adjectives and adverbs that end in any other consonant, add -ísimo/a.

fácil   facilísimo/a
¡La lección es facilísima!   (The lesson is very easy!)

Now try the practice exercises. Which set looks harder than the others?

YOUR TURN

Fill in the blanks with the correct comparative word. Use the cues in parentheses.

1. Emilia mira _____ televisión que Cristina. (*more*)
2. Tú eres _____ simpática que Catalina. (*less*)
3. No estudio _____ tú. (*as much as*)
4. Conocen _____ canciones que yo. (*more*)
5. Mi escuela es _____ que su escuela. (*better*)
6. Tu comes _____ comida como Ricardo. (*as much*)
7. La manzana es _____ rica que la banana. (*less*)
8. El hemano de Daniel es _____ que él. (*younger*)
9. La música clásica es _____ que el rock. (*worse*)
10. Mis padres tienen _____ dinero que mis tíos. (*more*)

Turn the following adjectives into superlatives. Use the cues.

11. paciente_____ (+)
12. diplomática_____ (–)
13. inteligente_____ (–)
14. bueno_____ (+)
15. vieja_____ (–)
16. malo_____ (+)
17. fácil_____ (+)
18. rápido_____ (–)
19. pequeño_____ (+)
20. caro_____ (–)

Turn the adjectives into absolute superlatives. Rewrite the sentences.

21. El pan (*bread*) es rico.
22. La niña es traviesa.
23. El profesor es malo.
24. La calle (*road*) es larga.
25. Estoy feliz.

14

CHAPTER 14
PREPOSITIONS

When we get home, the entire family is there, and Señora has prepared another of her fabulous meals. After the introductions to Señor and Señora, which Blair executes in perfect Spanish, of course, Ernesto extends his hand—needlessly, since they'd already met in the car.

"Blair, it is such a pleasure to welcome you to our house," he says in English.

"Oh, you speak English so well!" she squeals, twining her fingers through her perfectly curled blonde hair. Oh, *por favor*. Give me a break!

During lunch, Señor and Señora ask Blair questions about school and New York City, things they've never asked me in the past.

"Olivia," Señora says, "*Que suerte que tienes una amiga quien habla perfectament en español.*"[1] I look up, not quite understanding. Both Ernesto and Blair begin to translate for me at the same time. They both stop and laugh.

"I get it, I get it," I say.

After lunch, the three of us go in to watch *Los Niños*. I hadn't really planned on sharing our favorite show with Blair, but I can't exactly ask her to leave since I invited her. Blair sits between the two of us on the couch. I start to explain to Blair what the show is about, and how Doña Beatriz hid her jewel behind the portrait of Don John, and ever since then the painting has started to change to express the true evil and vice that Don John hides. But after a moment I realize Blair's not really listening. She's busy cozying up with Ernesto. Seems like Margo's not the only evil blond witch I have to worry about. . . .

PREPOSITIONS

We learned in Chapter 3 that a **preposition** expresses the relationship between things in terms of time or place. In other words, prepositions answer questions-

---

1   What luck that you have a friend who speaks Spanish so well.

like "where?" and "when?"

The examples we gave you were:

El vaso está en la mesa.	(The glass is on the table.)
Te veo antes de las 3:00.	(See you before 3:00.)

In the first example, the preposition *en* answers the question "where?" Where is the glass? It's on the table. In the second example, the preposition *antes de* answers "when?" When will I see you? Before 3:00.

Here are the most common prepositions:

a	at, to	**excepto**	except
ante	before	**hacia**	toward
bajo	under	**hasta**	to, up to, as far as, until
con	with	**para**	for
contra	against	**por**	for
de	of, from	**según**	according to
desde	from, since	**sin**	without
durante	during	**sobre**	on, over, about
en	in, into, on, at	**tras**	after
entre	between, among		

Prepositions cannot stand alone. They must be followed by a noun, a pronoun, or a verb in the infinitive. Take a look at these examples.

_{noun}
Salgo con <u>Ana</u>.   (I go out with Ana.)

_{pronoun}
Vamos con <u>ellos</u>.   (Let's go with them.)

_{infinitive verb}
Hace todo excepto <u>cocinar</u>.   (He does everything except cook.)

COMPOUND PREPOSITIONS

Prepositions can be grouped with adverbs or with other prepositions to form a single prepositional expression. Here are some of them.

además de	in addition to, besides	**detrás de**	after, behind
antes de	before	**encima de**	on, on top of, over
cerca de	near, close to	**enfrente de**	in front of, opposite
debajo de	under, beneath	**frente a**	in front of, opposite
delante de	in front of, before	**fuera de**	outside of, beyond
dentro de	inside, within	**lejos de**	far from
después de	after	**por delante de**	in front of

Examples:

Ella está delante de mí. (She is in front of me.)
Vivo cerca de la escuela. (I live close to school.)
Las llaves están encima de la mesa. (The keys are on top of the table.)

Prepositions often appear in phrases as well. Take a look at the following prepositional phrases.

a causa de	because of
acerca de	about, concerning
al lado de	next to, beside
en vez de	instead of
frente a	across from, opposite to

Examples:

Las tijeras están al lado del lápiz.
(The scissors are next to the pencil.)

Quiero hablar con la profesora acerca de mi nota.
(I want to talk to my teacher concerning my grade.)

INDIVIDUAL PREPOSITIONS

We won't kid you: Spanish prepositions are tough. Let's go over the tricky ones.

THE PREPOSITION A

You've already seen the preposition *a*, so this one shouldn't be too hard. Remember direct and indirect objects, covered way back in Chapter 12? If not, go back and review them briefly.

Now study the following rules for using the preposition *a*:

1. to introduce an indirect object

    Doy la manzana a Josefina.   (I give the apple to Josefina.)

2. to show movement toward something or some place

    Vamos a la cabaña.   (We're going to the cabin.)

3. to tell the time at which something happens

    El concierto es a las ocho.   (The concert is at eight o'clock.)

4. to show distance

    La escuela está a una cuadra.   (The school is one block away.)

5. when *alguien*, *nadie*, *alguno*, and *ninguno* are direct objects and refer to people

    No veo a nadie.   (I don't see anyone.)

6. to introduce a direct object that refers to a person

    Veo a mi hermana.   (I see my sister.)

7. to form the contraction *al* when *a* is followed by *el*

    Voy al (a + el) mercado.   (I am going to the supermarket.)

Now, to make matters even more complicated, there are certain verbs that are often accompanied by the preposition *a*. These are all followed by the verb in the infinitive. It's probably a good idea to go ahead and memorize them.

aprender a + infinitive (to learn to)	Aprendo a tocar el piano. (I learn how to play the piano.)
ayudar a + infinitive (to help)	Le ayudo a mi abuela. (I help my grandmother.)
comenzar a + infinitive (to begin to)	Comienza a llover. (It starts to rain.)
enseñar a + infinitive (to show how to)	Te enseño a cantar. (I teach you to sing.)
invitar a + infinitive (to invite to)	Lo invito al cine. (I invite him/her to the movies.)
ir a + infinitive (to go to)	Voy al supermercado. (I'm going to the supermarket.)

THE PREPOSITION *DE*

Use the preposition *de*:

1. to show possession

    La camisa es de Marta.   (The shirt is Marta's.)

2. to show nationality

    Soy de los Estados Unidos.   (I'm from the United States.)

3. to show the material that something is made of

    El plato es de plástico.   (The plate is made of plastic.)

4. to describe someone by something physical

    La señora de los ojos azules es mi madre.
    (The woman with blue eyes is my mother.)

5. to form the contraction *de* when *de* is followed by *el*

    Ella está hablando con el hombre del (de + el) restaurante.
    (She is speaking with the man from the restaurant.)

Here are some verbs that are often accompanied by *de*.

acabar de + infinitive (to have just done something)	Acabo de comer. (I just ate.)
dejar de + infinitive (to stop)	Quiero dejar de mentir. (I want to stop lying.)
pensar de (to think of)	¿Qué piensas del libro? (What do you think about the book?)
terminar de + infinitive (to finish)	Termino de lavar los platos. (I finish washing the dishes.)
tratar de + infinitive (to try to)	Trata de ayudarme. (He/She tries to help me.)

THE PREPOSITIONS *PARA* AND *POR*

The prepositions *para* and *por* can both be translated as "for." However, they have very different uses in Spanish.

Use the preposition *para*:

1. to indicate a particular use for which something is intended

    Las piernas son para caminar.   (Legs are for walking.)

2. to show the destination for which something is intended

    El regalo es para mi padre.   (The gift is for my father.)

3. with an infinitive that expresses the purpose of something

    Para comer, necesito un tenedor.   (To eat, I need a fork.)

4. to indicate a time at which something will be fulfilled, or a deadline

La entrada es para el concierto del domingo. (The ticket is for Sunday's concert.)

5. to indicate a comparison of inequality with something that is different from what is expected

Para extranjero, habla bien el español. (For a foreigner, he speaks Spanish well.)

Use the preposition *por*:

1. to indicate a length of time during which an action takes place

   ¿Me prestas el carro por dos días?   (Will you lend me the car for two days?)

2. to indicate movement through or along something

   El gato pasa por la ventana.   (The cat goes through the window.)

3. to indicate the means by which something is communicated

   Te llamo por teléfono.   (I call you on the phone.)

4. after the verbs *ir* (to go), *mandar* (to send), *enviar* (to mail), *volver* (to return), *regresar* (to come back), and *preguntar* (to ask for) when there is an object of an errand

   Te mando el paquete por avión.   (I send you the package airmail.)

5. to indicate the reason for an action

   Estoy en la universidad por mis padres.   (I'm in the university for the sake of my parents.)

6. to indicate a substitution (instead of)

   Yo corro por Manuel.   (I'm running in Manuel's place.)

7. to indicate an exchange of one thing for another

   Te doy diez dólares por la chaqueta.   (I'll give you ten dollars for the jacket.)

8. to indicate a unit of measurement

   El carro va ochenta kilómetros por hora.   (The car goes eighty kilometers per hour.)

VERBS WITHOUT PREPOSITIONS

The following verbs have prepositions in English, but none in Spanish. Don't let these confuse you.

agradecer (to be grateful for)	Te agradezco la ayuda. (I'm grateful to you for your help.)
buscar (to look for)	Busco mis llaves. (I'm looking for my keys.)
esperar (to wait for)	Los niños esperan el bus. (The kids are waiting for the bus.)
pedir + thing (to ask for something)	Pido un refresco. (I ask for a drink.)
pensar + infinitive (to plan on doing something)	Pienso ir a la playa. (I'm planning on going to the beach.)

Your head is probably reeling with prepositions now. Unfortunately, verbs can be learned, but prepositions must be memorized. In other words, logic does not always apply to prepositions. However, as you get more practice they'll become less of a challenge. Test your understanding by trying the following exercises.

YOUR TURN

Use the following compound prepositions to express where the cat is: *delante de, debajo de, encima de, dentro de, lejos de.* Write in complete sentences.

1.

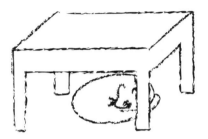

2.

3.

4.

5.

Choose the correct preposition. Write the letter in the space provided.

6. La mesa es _____ madera (*wood*).
   (A) a (B) de (C) No preposition.

7. Mando un mensaje a Arturo _____ correo electrónico (*email*).
   (A) para (B) por (C) en

8. La mantequilla (*butter*) es _____ el pan.
   (A) para (B) por (C) a

9. ¿Buscas _____ la clase de español?
   (A) a (B) para (C) No preposition

10. La película (*movie*) es _____ las tres de la tarde.
    (A) de (B) por (C) a

11. Ignacio corre _____ la esquina (*corner*).
    (A) de (B) hasta (C) No preposition

12. Espero _____ mi amiga Carla.
    (A) a (B) de (C) No preposition

13. La caja (*box*) es _____ los lápices.
    (A) por (B) con (C) para

15

CHAPTER 15
REFLEXIVE VERBS

The next day in class, Blair's practically bubbling over with enthusiasm.

"Guess what, Olivia? My father sent me two tickets to the *telenovela* awards show this Friday night in San José."

"Um, that's really nice for you, Blair" is about the best I can manage.

"I bet that Ernesto will be thrilled to go with me, don't you think? He's totally into that awful soap you guys watch, right? What *was* that, anyway? Oh, and thank you *so much* for inviting me back to your host family's. They are *so sweet!* Just wait until Ernesto sees the Dolce & Gabbana dress I bought to wear."

Well, at least I know when I'm defeated. Tickets to the *actual* awards show, as opposed to camping outside the red carpet with the rest of the plebs? Designer dresses? Blair totally knows the way to Ernesto's heart. If anyone can appreciate a slick dress, it's my glam pal, Ernesto. . . .

REFLEXIVE VERBS

At this point, we've gone over direct and indirect objects a couple of times. Remember that the direct object of a sentence is who or what receives the direct action of the verb. The indirect object of a sentence is who or what benefits, or is harmed by, the action of the verb.

When either the direct object or the indirect object of a sentence is the same person or thing as the subject, the sentence is **reflexive**. In other words, the action of the verb is "reflected" back to the subject.

Reflexive verbs are used to indicate that the subject is doing something to or for himself or herself.

A **reflexive verb** is identified by having -*se* attached to the infinitive.

lavarse	(to wash oneself)
levantarse	(to get up)

Here are some more reflexive verbs.

acostarse	to go to bed	**ponerse**	to put on
bañarse	to bathe	**preocuparse**	to worry about
cepillarse	to brush	**probarse**	to try on
despedirse de	to say good-bye to	**quedarse**	to stay
despertarse	to wake up	**quitarse**	to take off
dormirse	to go to sleep	**sentarse**	to sit down
llamarse	to be called/named	**sentirse**	to feel
peinarse	to comb one's hair	**vestirse**	to get dressed

REFLEXIVE PRONOUNS

Take a look at the following sentence. Do you see the pronoun? Reflexive verbs always use **reflexive pronouns**.

Yo me **lavo**. (I wash myself.)

reflexive pronoun

Here are the reflexive pronouns.

For the singular:

Person		
1st	**me**	myself
2nd	**te**	yourself
3rd	**se**	herself himself itself yourself (formal)

For the plural:

Person		
1st	nos	ourselves
2nd	os	yourselves
3rd	se	themselves yourselves (formal)

Reflexive pronouns follow the same rules for placement as object pronouns. They usually appear before the conjugated verb.

Examples:

Ellos se visten.	(They dress themselves.)
Yo me cepillo los dientes.	(I brush my teeth.)

In Spanish, unlike English, possessive pronouns (*mi, tu, su*, etc.) are not used with parts of the body.

María se lava la cara.	(María washes her face.)

STEM-CHANGING REFLEXIVE VERBS

Remember the stem-changing verbs from Chapter 6? Don't forget that the changes apply to reflexive verbs too.

Look at the list of reflexive verbs that we just gave you. From that list, can you identify the stem-changing verbs? They are:

·   *acostarse (o—ue)*

La niña se acuesta a las siete.	(The girl goes to bed at seven.)

·   *despedirse de (e—i)*

Me despido de mi abuela.	(I say good-bye to my grandmother.)

·   *dormirse (o—ue)*

Siempre me duermo en el bus.	(I always fall asleep on the bus.)

·   *probarse (o—ue)*

La muchacha se prueba el sombrero.	(The girl tries on the hat.)

·   *sentarse (e—ie)*

La mujer se sienta el la banca.   (The woman sits on the bench.)

- *sentirse (e—ie)*

    ¿Te sientes bién?   (Do you feel all right?)

- *vestirse (e—i)*

    El cura se viste de negro.   (The priest wears black.)

REFLEXIVE VERBS THAT EXPRESS CHANGE

Spanish also uses reflexive verbs to express a mental or physical change. In English, we would express such changes by "to get" or "to become." Take a look at the following examples.

aburrirse	to get bored	**desmayarse**	to faint
alegrarse	to become happy	**enfadarse**	to get angry
asustarse	to get scared	**enojarse**	to get angry
cansarse	to get tired	**resfriarse**	to catch a cold
casarse	to get married		

Examples:

No puedo ver sangre, porque me desmayo. (I can't see blood, because I faint.)

Rosa se asusta cuando ve un ratón. (Rosa gets scared when she sees a mouse.)

IDIOMATIC EXPRESSIONS
WITH REFLEXIVE VERBS

Some reflexive verbs have an idiomatic meaning. These verbs don't necessarily indicate an action done to or for oneself. However, their constructions are reflexive.

acordarse de	to remember	**olvidarse de**	to forget
arrepentirse de	to repent	**parecerse a**	to look like
atreverse a	to dare	**quejarse**	to complain
bularse de	to make fun of	**reírse**	to laugh at
irse	to go away	**tratarse de**	to be about

Examples:

¿Te acuerdas de Teodoro?   (Do you remember Teodoro?)
Los niños se burlan de la niña.   (The boys make fun of the girl.)

Now you've learned all about reflexive verbs and their corresponding pronouns. You've learned about reflexive verbs that express some sort of a physical change, and you've learned about reflexive verbs that appear in idiomatic expressions.

YOUR TURN

Translate the following sentences into Spanish.

1. I bathe myself every day.
2. Zoila tries on the shoes.
3. My father gets up at six o'clock in the morning.
4. The lady takes off her glasses (*lentes*).
5. Do you wash your face in the morning?
6. My best friend never takes off his hat.
7. Federico falls asleep at eleven o'clock.
8. The teacher sits on the desk (*escritorio*).

Use what you learned to fill in the gaps in these reflexive verb charts.

9. cansarse (to become tired)

Person	Singular	Plural
1st	yo _____	nosotros _____ nosotras _____
2nd	tú _____	vosotros _____ vosotras _____
3rd	él _____ ella _____ uted _____	ellos _____ ellas _____ ustedes _____

10. enojarse (to become angry)

Person	Singular	Plural
1st	yo _____	nosotros _____ nosotras _____
2nd	tú _____	vosotros _____ vosotras _____
3rd	él _____ ella _____ uted _____	ellos _____ ellas _____ ustedes _____

11. irse (to go away, to leave)

Person	Singular	Plural
1st	yo _____	nosotros _____ nosotras _____
2nd	tú _____	vosotros _____ vosotras _____
3rd	él _____ ella _____ uted _____	ellos _____ ellas _____ ustedes _____

12. reírse (to laugh)

Person	Singular	Plural
1st	yo _____	nosotros _____ nosotras _____
2nd	tú _____	vosotros _____ vosotras _____
3rd	él _____ ella _____ uted _____	ellos _____ ellas _____ ustedes _____

16

CHAPTER 16
PRETERITE TENSE

Later that day, I'm sitting on the opposite end of the sofa from Ernesto watching *Todos Los Niños*. I have to admit, I'm not only jealous of Blair, I'm also a bit annoyed with Ernesto. All the way home in the car he kept singing this dumb rap song under his breath, in a weird mix of his own accent and that of someone who grew up in Jamaica, Queens: "She got a *thing* for that Gucci that Fendi that Prada, / That BCBG, *Bur*berry, Dolce & Gabbana." But since those are like the only words he knows, he keeps singing them over and over.

"Ernesto, will you *please* stop singing that stupid song," I finally say.

"*No problemo, señorita,*" he says, his good mood completely unassailable. He goes right into humming some Ricky Martin song.

On our show, that hussy Margo has decided that Don Juan is the key to her quest to supplant Doña Beatriz, so she's really tramping it up and putting the moves on him, but he's staggering around so drunk he barely notices her. It's a pity—they're kind of perfect for each other.

"Margo actually looks . . . *caliente* today, no?"[1] says Ernesto.

Sigh. Men are such pigs. . . .

PRETERITE TENSE

Spanish uses two simple tenses to speak about the past: the preterite and the imperfect (Chapter 17).

---

1   hot

The **preterite tense** is used to express actions or states completed in the past.

Ayer fui al mercado. (Yesterday I went to the market.)

You'll learn more about when to use the preterite tense in Chapter 18.

REGULAR VERBS

In Chapter 5 we explained that all regular Spanish verbs have a stem that stays the same when the verb is conjugated. This holds true for the preterite tense. Let's look at stems again.

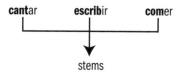

stems

To form the preterite tense of a regular verb, first drop the infinitive ending: -ar, -er, -ir, then add the following endings to the stem.

-AR VERBS

For singular -ar verbs, add -é, -aste, and -ó.

Person	Singular	
1st	yo canté	I sang
2nd	tú cantaste	you sang
3rd	él cantó	he sang
	ella cantó	she sang
	usted cantó	you sang (formal)

For plural -ar verbs, add -amos, -asteis, and -aron.

Person	Plural	
1st	nosotros cantamos	we sang (masculine)
	nosotras cantamos	we sang (feminine)
2nd	vosotros cantasteis	you sang (masculine)
	vosotras cantasteis	you sang (feminine)
3rd	ellos cantaron	they sang (masculine)
	ellas cantaron	they sang (feminine)
	ustedes cantaron	you sang (formal)

-ER AND -IR VERBS

For singular -er and -ir verbs, add -í, -iste, and -ió.

Person	Singular	
1st	yo comí	I ate
2nd	tú comiste	you ate
3rd	él comió	he ate
	ella comió	she ate
	usted comió	you ate (formal)

Person	Singular	
1st	yo escribí	I wrote
2nd	tú escribiste	you wrote
3rd	él escribió	he wrote
	ella escribió	she wrote
	usted escribió	you wrote (formal)

For plural -er and -ir verbs, add -imos, -isteis, and -ieron.

Person	Plural	
1st	nosotros comimos	we ate (masculine)
	nosotras comimos	we ate (feminine)
2nd	vosotros comisteis	you ate (masculine)
	vosotras comisteis	you ate (feminine)

3rd	ellos comieron	they ate (masculine)
	ellas comieron	they ate (feminine)
	ustedes comieron	you ate (formal)

Person		Plural
1st	nosotros escribimos	we wrote (masculine)
	nosotras escribimos	we wrote (feminine)
2nd	vosotros escribisteis	you wrote (masculine)
	vosotras escribisteis	you wrote (feminine)
3rd	ellos escribieron	they wrote (masculine)
	ellas escribieron	they wrote (feminine)
	ustedes escribieron	you wrote (formal)

STEM-CHANGING VERBS

Now, we have some good news. Remember all those stem-changing verbs you learned in the present tense? Luckily, for -ar and -er verbs this change does not happen in the preterite.

Examples:

- *cerrar* (to close)

    present: Ana cierra la puerta.   (Ana closes the door.)
    preterite: Ana cerró la puerta.   (Ana closed the door.)

- *volver* (to come back)

    present: Simón vuelve a las cinco.   (Simón comes back at five o'clock.)
    preterite: Simón volvió a las cinco.   (Simón came back at five o'clock.)

E-I

However, verbs that end in -ir and have a stem-change in the present tense have a stem-change in the preterite tense as well.

Verbs that have a stem-change from *e* to *ie* in the present tense have a stem-change in the third-person singular and the third-person plural of the preterite tense only. The change is from *e* to *i*.

PREFERIR (TO PREFER)

Person	Singular	
1st	yo preferí	I preferred
2nd	tú preferiste	you preferred
3nd	él prefirió	he preferred
	ella prefirió	she preferred
	usted prefirió	you preferred (formal)

Person	Plural	
1st	nosotros preferimos	we preferred (masculine)
	nosotras preferimos	we preferred (feminine)
2nd	vosotros preferisteis	you preferred (masculine)
	vosotras preferisteis	you preferred (feminine)
3rd	ellos prefirieron	they preferred (masculine)
	ellas prefirieron	they preferred (feminine)
	ustedes prefirieron	you preferred (formal)

There is another case in which a stem-change is from *e* to *i*. Verbs that have a stem-change from *e* to *i* in the present tense have a stem-change in the third-person singular and the third-person plural of the preterite tense.

VESTIR (TO DRESS)

Person	Singular	
1st	yo vestí	I dressed
2nd	tú vestiste	you dressed
3rd	él vistió	he dressed
	ella vistió	she dressed
	usted vistió	you dressed (formal)
Person	**Plural**	
1st	nosotros vestimos	we dressed (masculine)
	nosotras vestimos	we dressed (feminine)
2nd	vosotros vestisteis	you dressed (masculine)
	vosotras vestisteis	you dressed (feminine)
3rd	ellos vistieron	they dressed (masculine)
	ellas vistieron	they dressed (feminine)
	ustedes vistieron	you dressed (formal)

O-U

Similarly, verbs that have a stem-change from *o* to *ue* in the present tense have a stem-change in only the third-person singular and the third-person plural of the preterite tense. The change is from *o* to *u*.

DORMIR (TO SLEEP)

Person	Singular	
1st	yo dormí	I slept
2nd	tú dormiste	you slept
3rd	él durmió	he slept
	ella durmió	she slept
	usted durmió	you slept (formal)

Person	Plural	
1st	nosotros dormimos	we slept (masculine)
	nosotras dormimos	we slept (feminine)
2nd	vosotros dormisteis	you slept (masculine)
	vosotras dormisteis	you slept (feminine)
3rd	ellos durmieron	they slept (masculine)
	ellas durmieron	they slept (feminine)
	ustedes durmieron	you slept (formal)

VERBS WITH SPELLING CHANGES

There are other verbs that have slight spelling changes in the preterite form.

-CAR, -GAR, AND -ZAR VERBS

Verbs that end in -car, -gar, and -zar have changes in the first person singular of the preterite tense. These changes aren't arbitrary. As you will see, the changes preserve the sound of the consonant.

Verbs that end in -car change c to qu.

BUSCAR (TO LOOK FOR)

Person	Singular	
1st	yo busqué	I looked for
2nd	tú buscaste	you looked for
3rd	él buscó	he looked for
	ella buscó	she looked for
	usted buscó	you looked for (formal)

Verbs that end in -gar change g to gu.

LLEGAR (TO ARRIVE)

Person	Singular	
1st	yo llegué	I arrived
2nd	tú llegaste	you arrived
3rd	él llegó	he arrived
	ella llegó	she arrived
	usted llegó	you arrived (formal)

Verbs that end in -zar change z to c.

REZAR (TO PRAY)

Person	Singular	
1st	yo recé	I prayed
2nd	tú rezaste	you prayed
3rd	él rezó	he prayed
	ella rezó	she prayed
	usted rezó	you prayed (formal)

-AER, -EER, AND -UIR VERBS

Verbs that end in -aer, -eer, and -uir, as well as the verb oír (to hear) change i to y in the third-person singular and the third-person plural.

CAER (TO FALL)

Person		Singular
1st	yo caí	I fell
2nd	tú caíste	you fell
3rd	él cayó	he fell
	ella cayó	she fell
	usted cayó	you fell (formal)

Person		Plural
1st	nosotros caímos	we fell (masculine)
	nosotras caímos	we fell (feminine)
2nd	vosotros caísteis	you fell (masculine)
	vosotras caísteis	you fell (feminine)
3rd	ellos cayeron	they fell (masculine)
	ellas cayeron	they fell (feminine)
	ustedes cayeron	you fell (formal)

OÍR (TO HEAR)

Person		Singular
1st	yo oí	I heard
2nd	tú oíste	you heard
3rd	él oyó	he heard
	ella oyó	she heard
	usted oyó	you heard (formal)

Person		Plural
1st	nosotros oímos	we heard (masculine)
	nosotras oímos	we heard (feminine)
2nd	vosotros oísteis	you heard (masculine)
	vosotras oísteis	you heard (feminine)
3rd	ellos oyeron	they heard (masculine)
	ellas oyeron	they heard (feminine)
	ustedes oyeron	you heard (formal)

IRREGULAR VERBS

What verb tense would be complete without some irregulars?

U-STEM, *I*-STEM, *J*-STEM

Some pesky Spanish verbs have irregular stems in the preterite tense. However, they do share a common set of endings: -e, -iste, -o, -imos, -isteis, -ieron.

Here are some examples of verbs with irregular stems. Take a look at the verbs charts at the end of the book for their complete conjugations.

U-STEM:

andar	(anduv-)
estar	(estuv-)
tener	(tuv-)
poder	(pud-)
poner	(pus-)
saber	(sup-)

I-STEM:

hacer	(hic-)
querer	(quis-)
venir	(vin-)

J-STEM:

These verbs have a common irregular j-stem, but a different set of endings from those you have just learned: -e, -iste, -o, -imos, -isteis, -eron.

conducir	(conduj-)
decir	(dij-)
producir	(produj-)
traer	(traj-)

OTHER IRREGULARS

The verbs *dar* and *ver* take regular *-er* endings, but without the accents.

DAR (TO GIVE)

Person	Singular	
1st	yo di	I gave
2nd	tú diste	you gave
3rd	él dio	he gave
	ella dio	she gave
	usted dio	you gave (formal)

Person	Plural	
1st	nosotros dimos	we gave (masculine)
	nosotras dimos	we gave (feminine)
2nd	vosotros disteis	you gave (masculine)
	vosotras disteis	you gave (feminine)
3rd	ellos dieron	they gave (masculine)
	ellas dieron	they gave (feminine)
	ustedes dieron	you gave (formal)

VER (TO SEE)

Person	Singular	
1st	yo vi	I saw
2nd	tú viste	you saw
3rd	él vio	he saw
	ella vio	she saw
	usted vio	you saw (formal)

Person	Plural	
1st	nosotros vimos	we saw (masculine)
	nosotras vimos	we saw (feminine)
2nd	vosotros visteis	you saw (masculine)
	vosotras visteis	you saw (feminine)
3rd	ellos vieron	they saw (masculine)
	ellas vieron	they saw (feminine)
	ustedes vieron	you saw (formal)

IR (TO GO)/SER (TO BE)

The verbs *ir* and *ser* are identical in the preterite.

Person	Singular	
1st	yo fui	I went/was
2nd	tú fuiste	you went/were
3rd	él fue	he went/was
	ella fue	she went/was
	usted fue	you went/was (formal)

Person	Plural	
1st	nosotros fuimos	we went/were (masculine)
	nosotras fuimos	we went/were (feminine)
2nd	vosotros fuisteis	you went/were (masculine)
	vosotras fuisteis	you went/were (feminine)
3rd	ellos fueron	they went/were (masculine)
	ellas fueron	they went/were (feminine)
	ustedes fueron	you went/were (formal)

There's a lot to remember for preterites. However, once you start using them, you'll see that they come much more naturally than you think. It's just a matter of practice. Speaking of which, now that you're done with Chapter 16, you're ready to move on to the practice exercises.

YOUR TURN

Fill in the blanks with the preterite form of the verb in parentheses.

1. Mi tía Carlota _____ (vender) su carro.
2. Ayer yo _____ (comer) dos huevos fritos (*fried eggs*).
3. ¿Vosotros _____ (correr) en el parque?
4. Manuel, ¿ _____ (cerrar) la ventana (*window*)?
5. La niña _____ (vestir) a su muñeca (*doll*).
6. Ellos _____ (oír) un grito (*yell*) en el ático.
7. Yo _____ (llegar) tarde a la escuela.
8. El muchacho _____ (preferir) el helado (*ice cream*) de chocolate.
9. La señora _____ (rezar) en la iglesia.
10. Anoche nos _____ (dormir) a las diez.
11. Los perros ya _____ (salir).
12. Mi equipo (*team*) _____ (ganar) el campeonato (*championship*).

Conjugate the following verbs in the preterite tense.

13. yo _____ (dar)
14. nosotros _____ (ser)
15. vosotras _____ (ver)
16. tú _____ (conducir)
17. ellos _____ (producir)
18. él _____ (estar)
19. yo _____ (traer)
20. ella _____ (ir)
21. vosotros _____ (poder)
22. tú _____ (tener)
23. ustedes _____ (decir)
24. nosotros _____ (saber)

17

CHAPTER 17
IMPERFECT TENSE

So it's finally Friday, Ernesto's big day, and I come home to find him primping and preening over his vintage tuxedo, which is black and *satin,* with a faint pattern of black-on-black damask roses running across it.

"Um, are you sure you don't have that thing on inside out?" I tease him. But he actually looks fabulous. The tux is *totally* Ernesto.

"Hey, wise guy," he says, "the bathroom's free. You better go get ready."

"Ready for what?"

"What do you mean, 'ready for whaaat,'" he says, mimicking my American accent, and sort of sounding like a duck. "Ready for the awards show!"

"What are you talking about? You guys got a ticket for me?"

"Who needs a ticket? We're going to stake out the *alfombra roja,* scream like little girls at the actresses in their dresses, and then watch the show on TV at a cafe across the street. Go get glamorous."

"What about Blair?"

"Oh, it was very sweet of your *amiga bonita* to invite me,[1] but I very nicely told her no. She's just a little bit stuck on herself, you know? My big test with a girl is watching *Todos Los Niños* with her. If I can see she hates it, I know she takes herself too seriously to loosen up and have fun."

Ahem. It would seem that five years of watching *Passions* has at least prepared me for something!

IMPERFECT TENSE

Now that your brain is saturated with all the forms of the preterite, let's review

---

1   pretty friend

the second kind of simple past tense: the imperfect.

The **imperfect tense** is used to describe people, places, or things in the past.

> Cuando mi madre era joven, mis abuelos eran muy estrictos.
> (When my mother was young, my grandparents were very strict.)

It's also used to indicate an ongoing action in the past, as well as an action in the past that was never completed.

> Jaime esperaba en el garaje.   (Jaime was waiting in the garage.)

You'll learn more about the uses of the imperfect tense in the next chapter.

REGULAR VERBS

Luckily for you, all but three verbs have regular forms in the imperfect. Here's how you form them.

-AR VERBS

For singular *-ar* verbs, add *-aba*, *-abas*, and *-aba*.

Person	Singular	
1st	yo cantaba	I was singing
2nd	tú cantabas	you were singing
3rd	él cantaba	he was singing
	ella cantaba	she was singing
	usted cantaba	you were singing (formal)

For plural *-ar* verbs, add *-ábamos*, *-abais*, and *-aban.*

Person		Plural
1st	nosotros cantábamos	we were singing (masculine)
	nosotras cantábamos	we were singing (feminine)
2nd	vosotros cantabais	you were singing (masculine)
	vosotras cantabais	you were singing (feminine)
3rd	ellos cantaban	they were singing (masculine)
	ellas cantaban	they were singing (feminine)
	ustedes cantaban	you were singing (formal)

-ER AND -IR VERBS

For singular -er and -ir verbs, add -ía, -ías, and -ía.

Person		Plural
1st	yo comía	I was eating
2nd	tú comías	you were eating
3rd	él comía	he was eating
	ella comía	she was eating
	usted comía	you were eating (formal)

Person		Plural
1st	yo escribía	I was writing
2nd	tú escribías	you were writing
3rd	él escribía	he was writing
	ella escribía	she was writing
	usted escribía	you were writing (formal)

For plural -er and -ir verbs, add -íamos, -íais, and -ían.

Person		Plural
1st	nosotros comíamos	we were eating (masculine)
	nosotras comíamos	we were eating (feminine)
2nd	vosotros comíais	you were eating (masculine)
	vosotras comíais	you were eating (feminine)
3rd	ellos comían	they were eating (masculine)
	ellas comían	they were eating (feminine)
	ustedes comían	you were eating (formal)

Person		Plural
1st	nosotros escribíamos	we were writing (masculine)
	nosotras escribíamos	we were writing (feminine)
2nd	vosotros escribíais	you were writing (masculine)
	vosotras escribíais	you were writing (feminine)
3rd	ellos escribían	they were writing (masculine)
	ellas escribían	they were writing (feminine)
	ustedes escribían	you were writing (formal)

IRREGULAR VERBS

There are only three verbs that have irregular imperfect forms: *ir*, *ser*, and *ver*.

IR (TO GO)

Person		Singular
1st	yo iba	I was going
2nd	tú ibas	you were going
3rd	él iba	he was going
	ella iba	she was going
	usted iba	you were going (formal)

Person		Plural
1st	nosotros íbamos	we were going (masculine)
	nosotras íbamos	we were going (feminine)
2nd	vosotros ibais	you were going (masculine)
	vosotras ibais	you were going (feminine)
3rd	ellos iban	they were going (masculine)
	ellas iban	they were going (feminine)
	ustedes iban	you were going (formal)

SER (TO BE)

Person		Singular
1st	yo era	I was
2nd	tú eras	you were
3rd	él era	he was
	ella era	she was
	usted era	you were (formal)
Person		Plural
1st	nosotros éramos	we were (masculine)
	nosotras éramos	we were (feminine)
2nd	vosotros eráis	you were (masculine)
	vosotras eráis	you were (feminine)
3rd	ellos eran	they were (masculine)
	ellas eran	they were (feminine)
	ustedes eran	you were (formal)

VER (TO SEE)

Person		Singular
1st	yo veía	I was seeing
2nd	tú veías	you were seeing
3rd	él veía	he was seeing
	ella veía	she was seeing
	usted veía	you were seeing (formal)
Person		Plural
1st	nosotros veíamos	we were seeing (masculine)
	nosotras veíamos	we were seeing (feminine)
2nd	vosotros veíais	you were seeing (masculine)
	vosotras veíais	you were seeing (feminine)
3rd	ellos veían	they were seeing (masculine)
	ellas veían	they were seeing (feminine)
	ustedes veían	you were seeing (formal)

That's it for the imperfect tense. Before you complete the following exercises, review both the preterite and the imperfect tenses.

YOUR TURN

Conjugate the following verbs in the imperfect tense.

1. vosotros _____ (ir)
2. tú _____ recibir)
3. yo _____ (ser)
4. los estudiantes _____ (leer)
5. vosotros _____ (ver)
6. ellas _____ (correr)
7. mi padres _____ (ir)
8. vosotras _____ (ser)
9. tú _____ (tener)
10. nosotros _____ (llegar)

Fill in the blanks with the imperfect form of the verb in parentheses.

11. Magdalena _____ (ver) la televisión todos los días.
12. El año pasado (*last year*), mis tareas _____ (ser) muy difíciles.
13. José se _____ (aburrir) en la clase de español.
14. Francisco me _____ (esperar) en el gimnasio.
15. En el año 1997, nosotros _____ (ser) muy pequeños.
16. Hace veinte años (*twenty years ago*), mi ciudad _____ (ser) más limpia (*clean*).
17. El verano pasado (*last summer*) vosotros _____ (leer) todos los días.
18. Tú siempre _____ (mandar) cartas a tus abuelos.
19. Los niños se _____ (bañar) en la piscina (*swimming pool*).
20. Cuando yo _____ (vivir) en Quito, yo _____ (ir) siempre al Mitad del Mundo.

18

CHAPTER 18
PRETERITE OR IMPERFECT

The red carpet is everything Ernesto promised, and more. Elvira (Doña B) shows up in the most amazing dress. It's canary yellow, sequined, slit up the side, plunging neckline (the dramatic cleavage being quite a change from her demure eighteenth-century attire), and a hat with about three feet of yellow feathers sticking out of it. All the actresses look so *different* in their glamour gowns from their personas on the *telenovelas*.

Even the actress who plays Margo looks fantastic out of her chambermaid-witch costume. Her dress is a brilliant blue sheath decorated with rhinestones. It occurs to me that red would have suited her better, but then she flashes us a brilliant smile, and I suddenly forget about wanting to drop her crystal ball on her head.

Next to us someone rolls their eyes and complains, "*Amarillo y azul, amarillo y azul. . . .*"[1] And it's true—two thirds of the actresses *are* wearing *amarillo* or *azul.* I turn to comment on this to Ernesto, but with a shock I realize he's talking to Big Bird, then I realize it's not *really* a seven-foot bird, it's Doña Beatriz shaking his hand and soaking up our adoration. She reaches across the rope, takes Ernesto's autograph book, signs it, and moves back up the red carpet at a stately pace.

Ernesto and I take one look at each other and start jumping up and down and screaming like ten-year-old girls at a Britney Spears concert.

---

1   Yellow and blue, yellow and blue. . . .

PRETERITE OR IMPERFECT?

Once you have determined that you need to use a past tense verb, you have to decide whether to use the preterite or the imperfect. To do this, try to visualize the perspective given to the verb in its specific context. In other words, think about the action of the verb.

USE THE PRETERITE

Does the verb express an action that has a specific ending? Was the action completed? In this case, use the preterite tense.

> La hermana de Paul se casó el año pasado.
> (Paul's sister got married last year.)

In the sentence above, the verb is in the preterite tense. The action of Paul's sister getting married happened at that moment and was then over.

Does the verb express the beginning or end of a past action? Then use the preterite tense.

La película empezó a las diez.	(The movie started at ten.)
Ayer terminé el proyecto.	(Yesterday I finished the project.)

In the first sentence, the movie had a specific start time: ten o'clock. In the second sentence, the project was finished at a specific time: yesterday.

Does the verb narrate a series of past actions or events? Then use the preterite tense. Take a look at the following sentence.

> La señora paró el carro, abrió la ventana, y gritó al niño.
> (The lady stopped the car, opened the window, and shouted at the boy.)

USE THE IMPERFECT

Does the verb express an action that was habitual? Then use the imperfect tense.

> Carlos caminaba todas las tardes por una hora.
> (Carlos walked for an hour every afternoon.)

In the sentence above, the verb is in the imperfect tense. The action was habitual: Carlos walked every afternoon for an hour.

Does the verb describe an ongoing past event with no definite beginning or end? Then use the imperfect tense.

> María Clara conducía muy rápido en la ciudad.
> (María Clara drove very fast in the city.)

Does the verb describe a mental, physical, or emotional state or condition? Then use the imperfect tense.

> La chica se sentía mal.
> (The girl felt ill./The girl was feeling ill.)

> Los hombres eran altos y tenían ojos verdes.
> (The men were tall and they had green eyes.)

In both sentences, the verb is expressing some sort of a physical condition. The first sentence expresses how the girl was feeling, and the second sentence expresses what the men looked like.

USE THE PRETERITE AND THE IMPERFECT

In some cases, you can use both the preterite and the imperfect tenses in the same sentence. In this case, the imperfect tense describes what was happening, while the preterite tense describes the action that interrupted.

> what was happening   interrupting action
> Catalina <u>hablaba</u> por teléfono cuando <u>sonó</u> el timbre.
> (Catalina was speaking on the phone when the doorbell rang.)

In the sentence above, the action of the doorbell ringing interrupted Catalina's talking.

Sometimes you will see the preterite and the imperfect tenses together in long news or fiction stories. In these cases, the imperfect tense gives us all the background information, such as the time, weather, and location, while the preterite tense tells us what happened. Take a look at the following narrative.

> Era medianoche, y caía la lluvia. Hacía mucho frío,
> pero salí de todas maneras. De repente, me resbalé
> en un charco de agua y caí en la vereda. ¡Ay!

(It was midnight, and it was raining. It was very cold,
but I went out anyway. Suddenly, I slipped on a puddle of water
and fell on the sidewalk. Ouch!)

VERBS THAT CHANGE MEANING

There are some verbs that actually change meaning when they are used in the preterite tense. Take a look at the following examples.

SABER

When *saber* is in the imperfect tense, it means "to know."

Sabía español cuando era niño.   (He knew Spanish as a child.)

When saber is in the preterite tense, it means "to be informed, to find out."

Supo que su madre murió.   (He found out that his mother died.)

CONOCER

When conocer is in the imperfect tense, it means "to know."

Conocíamos a la familia García.   (We knew the García family.)

When conocer is in the preterite tense, it means "to meet for the first time."

Conocí a Magdalena en la fiesta.   (I met Magdalena at the party.)

QUERER

When *querer* is in the imperfect tense, it means "to want."

Queríamos viajar.   (We wanted to travel.)

When *querer* is in the preterite tense, it can either mean "to attempt" or "to refuse to."

Quiso escapar, pero no pudo.   (He tried to escape, but he couldn't.)
No quiso ayudarme.   (He refused to help me.)

In the past few chapters you've learned how and when to use both the preterite tense and the imperfect tense. You've learned how to conjugate them and what situations call for which tense. Let's try some practice exercises.

YOUR TURN

Choose the verb tense, based on the context of the sentence. Write the letter in the space provided.

1. Todos los días, los novios _____ juntos.
   (A) almorzaron (B) almorzaban

2. Francisco y yo _____ al parque ayer.
   (A) íbamos (B) fuimos

3. Hoy _____ a casa a las dos de la tarde.
   (A) regresamos (B) regresábamos

4. Cristina tocaba la guitarra cuando_____ el teléfono.
   (A) sonaba (B) sonó

5. La profesora _____ la lección.
   (A) comenzó (B) comenzaba

6. Llegué a casa, comí, y _____ mi libro.
   (A) leía (B) leí

Fill in the blank with the preterite or imperfect tense of the verb in parentheses.

7. Esta mañana Paco _____ (levantarse) temprano.

8. Cuando yo _____ (ser) niña, _____ (creer) en Santa Claus.

9. Para mi cumpleaños María me _____ (dar) dos muñecas.

10. De repente _____ (empezar) a caer nieve.

11. El niño _____ (llorar) todas las noches.

12. Cuando yo _____ (entrar) al cuarto, _____ (ver) a mi hermano.

13. En los años sesenta ese hombre _____ (ser) un cantante famoso.

14. Ayer Nancy _____ (comer) una ensalada.

15. La profesora _____ (olvidarse) su pluma en la clase.

16. Anoche _____ (hacer) mucho frío.

19

CHAPTER 19
EPILOGUE

Here I am again, back in my old Spanish I classroom in New York. It's fall now, and the leaves are beginning to turn. Class is almost finished for the day. Profesora is at the board, writing out the differences between preterite and imperfect for what seems like the fiftieth time. I look around the class to see who's not paying attention. All of the kids have their Spanish name on a card taped to the front of their desks.

"José?" I call out. "José, ¿Qué haces?"[1] I ask. José looks startled. He was gazing out the window. Profesora turns around from the blackboard and looks at me. I walk over and pull up a chair next to John's desk while she continues with the lesson.

"José? John? Tell me what you don't understand."

You see, I'm not in Spanish I as a student any more. I'm there as a tutor. After Costa Rica, I came back and took Profesora's test and passed with flying colors. I was acing Spanish II, too, without really trying, and so Profesora asked if I might also be willing to help out with her Spanish I class, for extra credit, of course. While it meant giving up *Passions,* as I would never be able to leave school just as class ended as I did last year, I agreed to do it. I think that's something I learned from Ernesto: Sometimes real life is better than the TV version.

I still tape *Passions,* though. I mean, you can't expect miracles, can you?

VERB CHARTS

Here are the verbs that you've studied in this book along with some others that you will encounter in your studies. As you will see, we've left out the subject pronouns. If you remember from your lessons, the subject pronouns aren't always necessary. Context and verb endings will allow you to identify the subject of the verbs.

---

1   What are you doing?

Don't forget your subject pronouns, though. Here they are again.

Person	Singular	Plural
1st	yo	nosotros nosotras
2nd	tú	vosotros vosotras
3rd	él ella usted	ellos ellas ustedes

ABRIR (TO OPEN)

PRESENT		PRETERITE		IMPERFECT	
abro	abrimos	abrí	abrimos	abría	abríamos
abres	abrís	abriste	abristeis	abrías	abríais
abre	abren	abrió	abrieron	abría	abrían

ACTUAR (TO ACT, TO BEHAVE)

PRESENT		PRETERITE		IMPERFECT	
actúo	actuamos	actué	actuamos	actuaba	actuábamos
actúas	actuáis	actuaste	actuasteis	actuabas	actuabais
actúa	actúan	actuó	actuaron	actuaba	actuaban

ALMORZAR (TO HAVE LUNCH)

PRESENT		PRETERITE		IMPERFECT	
almuerzo	almorzamos	almorcé	almorzamos	almorzaba	almorzábamos
almuerzas	almorzáis	almorzaste	almorzasteis	almorzabas	almorzabais
almuerza	almuerzan	almorzó	almorzaron	almorzaba	almorzaban

ANDAR (TO WALK, TO GO)

PRESENT		PRETERITE		IMPERFECT	
ando	andamos	anduve	anduvimos	andaba	andábamos
andas	andáis	anduviste	anduvisteis	andabas	andabais
anda	andan	anduvo	anduvieron	andaba	andaban

APRENDER (TO LEARN)

PRESENT		PRETERITE		IMPERFECT	
aprendo	aprendemos	aprendí	aprendimos	aprendía	aprendíamos
aprendes	aprendéis	aprendiste	aprendisteis	aprendías	aprendíais
aprende	aprenden	aprendió	aprendieron	aprendía	aprendían

BUSCAR (TO SEARCH FOR, TO LOOK FOR)

PRESENT		PRETERITE		IMPERFECT	
busco	buscamos	busqué	buscamos	buscaba	buscábamos
buscas	buscáis	buscaste	buscasteis	buscabas	buscabais
busca	buscan	buscó	buscaron	buscaba	buscaban

C

CAER (TO FALL)

PRESENT		PRETERITE		IMPERFECT	
caigo	caemos	caí	caímos	caía	caíamos
caes	caéis	caíste	caísteis	caías	caíais
cae	caen	cayó	cayeron	caía	caían

CANTAR (TO SING)

PRESENT		PRETERITE		IMPERFECT	
canto	cantamos	canté	cantamos	cantaba	cantábamos
cantas	cantáis	cantaste	cantasteis	cantabas	cantabais
canta	cantan	cantó	cantaron	cantaba	cantaban

CERRAR (TO CLOSE)

PRESENT		PRETERITE		IMPERFECT	
cierro	cerramos	cerré	cerramos	cerraba	cerrábamos
cierras	cerráis	cerraste	cerrasteis	cerrabas	cerrabais
cierra	cierran	cerró	cerraron	cerraba	cerraban

COMER (TO EAT)

PRESENT		PRETERITE		IMPERFECT	
como	comemos	comí	comimos	comía	comíamos
comes	coméis	comiste	comisteis	comías	comíais
come	comen	comió	comieron	comía	comían

COMPONER (TO FIX, TO REPAIR)

PRESENT		PRETERITE		IMPERFECT	
compongo	componemos	compuse	compusimos	componía	componíamos
compones	componéis	compusiste	compusisteis	componías	componíais
compone	componen	compuso	compusieron	componía	componían

COMPRENDER (TO UNDERSTAND, TO COMPREHEND)

PRESENT		PRETERITE	
comprendo	comprendemos	comprendí	comprendimos
comprendes	comprendéis	comprendiste	comprendisteis
comprende	comprenden	comprendió	comprendieron

IMPERFECT	
comprendía	comprendíamos
comprendías	comprendíais
comprendía	comprendían

CONDUCIR (TO DRIVE)

PRESENT		PRETERITE		IMPERFECT	
conduzco	conducimos	conduje	condujimos	conducía	conducíamos
conduces	conducís	condujiste	condujisteis	conducías	conducíais
conduce	conducen	condujo	condujeron	conducía	conducían

CONFIAR (TO CONFIDE, TO TRUST)

PRESENT		PRETERITE		IMPERFECT	
confío	confiamos	confié	confiamos	confiaba	confiábamos
confías	confiáis	confiaste	confiasteis	confiabas	confiabais
confía	confían	confió	confiaron	confiaba	confiaban

CONOCER (TO KNOW, TO RECOGNIZE)

PRESENT		PRETERITE		IMPERFECT	
conozco	conocemos	conocí	conocimos	conocía	conocíamos
conoces	conocéis	conociste	conocisteis	conocías	conocíais
conoce	conocen	conoció	conocieron	conocía	conocían

CONTAR (TO COUNT, TO TELL)

PRESENT		PRETERITE		IMPERFECT	
cuento	contamos	conté	contamos	contaba	contábamos
cuentas	contáis	contaste	contasteis	contabas	contabais
cuenta	cuentan	contó	contaron	contaba	contaban

CONTINUAR (TO CONTINUE)

PRESENT		PRETERITE	
continúo	continuamos	continué	continuamos
continúas	continuáis	continuaste	continuasteis
continúa	continúan	continuó	continuaron

IMPERFECT	
continuaba	continuábamos
continuabas	continuabais
continuaba	continuaban

CORRER (TO RUN)

PRESENT		PRETERITE		IMPERFECT	
corro	corremos	corrí	corrimos	corría	corríamos
corres	corréis	corriste	corristeis	corrías	corríais
corre	corren	corrió	corrieron	corría	corrían

COSTAR (TO COST)

PRESENT		PRETERITE		IMPERFECT	
cuesta	cuestan	costó	costaron	costaba	costaban

D

DAR (TO GIVE)

PRESENT		PRETERITE		IMPERFECT	
doy	damos	di	dimos	daba	dábamos
das	dais	diste	disteis	dabas	dabais
da	dan	dio	dieron	daba	daban

DECIR (TO SAY, TO TELL)

PRESENT		PRETERITE		IMPERFECT	
digo	decimos	dije	dijimos	decía	decíamos
dices	decís	dijiste	dijisteis	decías	decíais
dice	dicen	dijo	dijeron	decía	decían

DEFENDER (TO DEFEND)

PRESENT		PRETERITE		IMPERFECT	
defiendo	defendemos	defendí	defendimos	defendía	defendíamos
defiendes	defendéis	defendiste	defendisteis	defendías	defendíais
defiende	defienden	defendió	defendieron	defendía	defendían

DESPERTAR (TO WAKE)

PRESENT		PRETERITE		IMPERFECT	
despierto	despertamos	desperté	despertamos	despertaba	despertábamos
despiertas	despertáis	despertaste	despertasteis	despertabas	despertabais
despierta	despiertan	despertó	despertaron	despertaba	despertaban

DESTRUIR (TO DESTROY)

PRESENT		PRETERITE		IMPERFECT	
destruyo	destruimos	destruí	destruimos	destruía	destruíamos
destruyes	destruís	destruiste	destruisteis	destruías	destruíais
destruye	destruyen	destruyó	destruyeron	destruía	destruían

DEVOLVER (TO RETURN)

PRESENT		PRETERITE		IMPERFECT	
devuelvo	devolvemos	devolví	devolvimos	devolvía	devolvíamos
devuelves	devolvéis	devolviste	devolvisteis	devolvías	devolvíais
devuelve	devuelven	devolvió	devolvieron	devolvía	devolvían

DISTRIBUIR (TO DISTRIBUTE)

PRESENT		PRETERITE		IMPERFECT	
distribuyo	distribuimos	distribuí	distribuimos	distribuía	distribuíamos
distribuyes	distribuís	distribuiste	distribuisteis	distribuías	distribuíais
distribuye	distribuyen	distribuyó	distribuyeron	distribuía	distribuían

DORMIR (TO SLEEP)

PRESENT		PRETERITE		IMPERFECT	
duermo	dormimos	dormí	dormimos	dormía	dormíamos
duermes	dormís	dormiste	dormisteis	dormías	dormíais
duerme	duermen	durmió	durmieron	dormía	dormían

EMPEZAR (TO START, TO BEGIN)

PRESENT		PRETERITE		IMPERFECT	
empiezo	empezamos	empecé	empezamos	empezaba	empezábamos
empiezas	empezáis	empezaste	empezasteis	empezabas	empezabais
empieza	empiezan	empezó	empezaron	empezaba	empezaban

ENTENDER (TO UNDERSTAND)

PRESENT		PRETERITE		IMPERFECT	
entiendo	entendemos	entendí	entendimos	entendía	entendíamos
entiendes	entendéis	entendiste	entendisteis	entendías	entendíais
entiende	entienden	entendió	entendieron	entendía	entendían

ENVIAR (TO SEND)

PRESENT		PRETERITE		IMPERFECT	
envío	enviamos	envié	enviamos	enviaba	enviábamos
envías	enviáis	enviaste	enviasteis	enviabas	enviabais
envía	envían	envió	enviaron	enviaba	enviaban

ESCRIBIR (TO WRITE)

PRESENT		PRETERITE		IMPERFECT	
escribo	escribimos	escribí	escribimos	escribía	escribíamos
escribes	escribís	escribiste	escribisteis	escribías	escribíais
escribe	escriben	escribió	escribieron	escribía	escribían

ESTAR (TO BE)

PRESENT		PRETERITE		IMPERFECT	
estoy	estamos	estuve	estuvimos	estaba	estábamos
estás	estáis	estuviste	estuvisteis	estabas	estabais
está	están	estuvo	estuvieron	estaba	estaban

ESTUDIAR (TO STUDY)

PRESENT		PRETERITE		IMPERFECT	
estudio	estudiamos	estudié	estudiamos	estudiaba	estudiábamos
estudias	estudiáis	estudiaste	estudiasteis	estudiabas	estudiabais
estudia	estudian	estudió	estudiaron	estudiaba	estudiaban

G

GUIAR (TO GUIDE, TO LEAD)

PRESENT		PRETERITE		IMPERFECT	
guío	guiamos	guié	guiamos	guiaba	guiábamos
guías	guiáis	guiaste	guiasteis	guiabas	guiabais
guía	guían	guió	guiaron	guiaba	guiaban

H

HABER (TO HAVE)

PRESENT		PRETERITE		IMPERFECT	
he	hemos	hube	hubimos	había	habíamos
has	habéis	hubes	hubisteis	habías	habíais
ha	han	hubo	hubieron	había	habían

HACER (TO DO, TO MAKE)

PRESENT		PRETERITE		IMPERFECT	
hago	hacemos	hice	hicimos	hacía	hacíamos
haces	hacéis	hiciste	hicisteis	hacías	hacíais
hace	hacen	hizo	hicieron	hacía	hacían

I

INCLUIR (TO INCLUDE)

PRESENT		PRETERITE		IMPERFECT	
incluyo	incluimos	incluí	incluimos	incluía	incluíamos
incluyes	incluís	incluiste	incluisteis	incluías	incluíais
incluye	incluyen	incluyó	incluyeron	incluía	incluían

IR (TO GO)

PRESENT		PRETERITE		IMPERFECT	
voy	vamos	fui	fuimos	iba	íbamos
vas	vais	fuiste	fuisteis	ibas	ibais
va	van	fue	fueron	iba	iban

L

LEER (TO READ)

PRESENT		PRETERITE		IMPERFECT	
leo	leemos	leí	leímos	leía	leíamos
lees	leéis	leíste	leísteis	leías	leíais
lee	leen	leyó	leyeron	leía	leían

LL

LLEGAR (TO ARRIVE)

PRESENT		PRETERITE		IMPERFECT	
llego	llegamos	llegué	llegamos	llegaba	llegábamos
llegas	llegáis	llegaste	llegasteis	llegabas	llegabais
llega	llegan	llegó	llegaron	llegaba	llegaban

LLEVAR (TO TAKE)

PRESENT		PRETERITE		IMPERFECT	
llevo	llevamos	llevé	llevamos	llevaba	llevábamos
llevas	lleváis	llevaste	llevasteis	llevabas	llevabais
lleva	llevan	llevó	llevaron	llevaba	llevaban

M

MENTIR (TO LIE)

PRESENT		PRETERITE		IMPERFECT	
miento	mentimos	mentí	mentimos	mentía	mentíamos
mientes	mentís	mentiste	mentisteis	mentías	mentíais
miente	mienten	mintió	mintieron	mentía	mentían

MOVER (TO MOVE)

PRESENT		PRETERITE		IMPERFECT	
muevo	movemos	moví	movimos	movía	movíamos
mueves	molvéis	moviste	movisteis	movías	movíais
mueve	mueven	movió	movieron	movía	movían

OÍR (TO HEAR)

PRESENT		PRETERITE		IMPERFECT	
oigo	oímos	oí	oímos	oía	oíamos
oyes	oís	oíste	oísteis	oías	oíais
oye	oyen	oyó	oyeron	oía	oían

PARECER (TO APPEAR, TO RESEMBLE)

PRESENT		PRETERITE		IMPERFECT	
parezco	parecemos	parecí	parecimos	parecía	parecíamos
pareces	parecéis	pareciste	parecisteis	parecías	parecíais
parece	parecen	pareció	parecieron	parecía	parecían

PEDIR (TO ASK FOR, TO REQUEST)

PRESENT		PRETERITE		IMPERFECT	
pido	pedimos	pedí	pedimos	pedía	pedíamos
pides	pedís	pediste	pedisteis	pedías	pedíais
pide	piden	pidió	pidieron	pedía	pedían

PENSAR (TO THINK)

PRESENT		PRETERITE		IMPERFECT	
pienso	pensamos	pensé	pensamos	pensaba	pensábamos
piensas	pensáis	pensaste	pensasteis	pensabas	pensabais
piensa	piensan	pensó	pensaron	pensaba	pensaban

PERDER (TO LOSE)

PRESENT		PRETERITE		IMPERFECT	
pierdo	perdemos	perdí	perdimos	perdía	perdíamos
pierdes	perdéis	perdiste	perdisteis	perdías	perdíais
pierde	pierden	perdió	perdieron	perdía	perdían

PODER (TO BE ABLE TO)

PRESENT		PRETERITE		IMPERFECT	
puedo	podemos	pude	pudimos	podía	podíamos
puedes	podéis	pudiste	pudisteis	podías	podíais
puede	pueden	pudo	pudieron	podía	podían

PONER (TO PUT)

PRESENT		PRETERITE		IMPERFECT	
pongo	ponemos	puse	pusimos	ponía	poníamos
pones	ponéis	pusiste	pusisteis	ponías	poníais
pone	ponen	puso	pusieron	ponía	ponían

PREFERIR (TO PREFER)

PRESENT		PRETERITE		IMPERFECT	
prefiero	preferimos	preferí	preferimos	prefería	preferíamos
prefieres	preferís	preferiste	preferisteis	preferías	preferíais
prefiere	prefieren	prefirió	prefirieron	prefería	preferían

PREPARAR (TO PREPARE)

PRESENT		PRETERITE		IMPERFECT	
preparo	preparamos	preparé	preparamos	preparaba	preparábamos
preparas	preparáis	preparaste	preparasteis	preparabas	preparabais
prepara	preparan	preparó	prepararon	preparaba	preparaban

PRODUCIR (TO PRODUCE)

PRESENT		PRETERITE		IMPERFECT	
produzco	producimos	produje	produjimos	producía	producíamos
produces	producís	produjiste	produjisteis	producías	producíais
produce	producen	produjo	produjeron	producía	producían

QUERER (TO WANT)

PRESENT		PRETERITE		IMPERFECT	
quiero	queremos	quise	quisimos	quería	queríamos
quieres	queréis	quisiste	quisisteis	querías	queríais
quiere	quieren	quiso	quisieron	quería	querían

RECORDAR (TO REMEMBER)

PRESENT		PRETERITE		IMPERFECT	
recuerdo	recordamos	recordé	recordamos	recordaba	recordábamos
recuerdas	recordáis	recordaste	recordasteis	recordabas	recordabais
recuerda	recuerdan	recordó	recordaron	recordaba	recordaban

REGRESAR (TO RETURN, TO COME BACK)

PRESENT		PRETERITE		IMPERFECT	
regreso	regresamos	regresé	regresamos	regresaba	regresábamos
regresas	regresáis	regresaste	regresasteis	regresabas	regresabais
regresa	regresan	regresó	regresaron	regresaba	regresaban

REPETIR (TO REPEAT)

PRESENT		PRETERITE		IMPERFECT	
repito	repetimos	repetí	repetimos	repetía	repetíamos
repites	repetís	repetiste	repetisteis	repetías	repetíais
repite	repiten	repitió	repitieron	repetía	repetían

REZAR (TO PRAY)

PRESENT		PRETERITE		IMPERFECT	
rezo	rezamos	recé	rezamos	rezaba	rezábamos
rezas	rezáis	rezaste	rezasteis	rezabas	rezabais
reza	rezan	rezó	rezaron	rezaba	rezaban

S

SABER (TO KNOW)

PRESENT		PRETERITE		IMPERFECT	
sé	sabemos	supe	supimos	sabía	sabíamos
sabes	sabéis	supiste	supisteis	sabías	sabíais
sabe	saben	supo	supieron	sabía	sabían

SACAR (TO TAKE OUT)

PRESENT		PRETERITE		IMPERFECT	
saco	sacamos	saqué	sacamos	sacaba	sacábamos
sacas	sacáis	sacaste	sacasteis	sacabas	sacabais
saca	sacan	sacó	sacaron	sacaba	sacaban

SALIR (TO GO OUT, TO EXIT)

PRESENT		PRETERITE		IMPERFECT	
salgo	salimos	salí	salimos	salía	salíamos
sales	salís	saliste	salisteis	salías	salíais
sale	salen	salió	salieron	salía	salían

SALUDAR (TO GREET)

PRESENT		PRETERITE		IMPERFECT	
saludo	saludamos	saludé	saludamos	saludaba	saludábamos
saludas	saludáis	saludaste	saludasteis	saludabas	saludabais
saluda	saludan	saludó	saludaron	saludaba	saludaban

SENTIR (TO FEEL)

PRESENT		PRETERITE		IMPERFECT	
siento	sentimos	sentí	sentimos	sentía	sentíamos
sientes	sentís	sentiste	sentisteis	sentías	sentíais
siente	sienten	sintió	sintieron	sentía	sentían

SER (TO BE)

PRESENT		PRETERITE		IMPERFECT	
soy	somos	fui	fuimos	era	éramos
eres	sois	fuiste	fuisteis	eras	erais
es	son	fue	fueron	era	eran

SERVIR (TO SERVE)

PRESENT		PRETERITE		IMPERFECT	
sirvo	servimos	serví	servimos	servía	servíamos
sirves	servís	serviste	servisteis	servías	servíais
sirve	sirven	sirvió	sirvieron	servía	servían

SUPONER (TO SUPPOSE)

PRESENT		PRETERITE		IMPERFECT	
supongo	suponemos	supuse	supusimos	suponía	suponíamos
supones	suponéis	supusiste	supusisteis	suponías	suponíais
supone	suponen	supuso	supusieron	suponía	suponían

T

TENER (TO HAVE)

PRESENT		PRETERITE		IMPERFECT	
tengo	tenemos	tuve	tuvimos	tenía	teníamos
tienes	tenéis	tuviste	tuvisteis	tenías	teníais
tiene	tienen	tuvo	tuvieron	tenía	tenían

TOMAR (TO DRINK, TO TAKE)

PRESENT		PRETERITE		IMPERFECT	
tomo	tomamos	tomé	tomamos	tomaba	tomábamos
tomas	tomáis	tomaste	tomasteis	tomabas	tomabais
toma	toman	tomó	tomaron	tomaba	tomaban

TRAER (TO BRING)

PRESENT		PRETERITE		IMPERFECT	
traigo	traemos	traje	trajimos	traía	traíamos
traes	traéis	trajiste	trajisteis	traías	traíais
trae	traen	trajo	trajeron	traía	traían

V

VENIR (TO COME)

PRESENT		PRETERITE		IMPERFECT	
vengo	venimos	vine	vinimos	venía	veníamos
vienes	venís	viniste	vinisteis	venías	veníais
viene	vienen	vino	vinieron	venía	venían

VER (TO SEE)

PRESENT		PRETERITE		IMPERFECT	
veo	vemos	vi	vimos	veía	veíamos
ves	veis	viste	visteis	veías	veíais
ve	ven	vio	vieron	veía	veían

VESTIR (TO DRESS)

PRESENT		PRETERITE		IMPERFECT	
visto	vestimos	vestí	vestimos	vestía	vestíamos
vistes	vestís	vestiste	vestisteis	vestías	vestíais
viste	visten	vistió	vistieron	vestía	vestían

VIVIR (TO LIVE)

PRESENT		PRETERITE		IMPERFECT	
vivo	vivimos	viví	vivimos	vivía	vivíamos
vives	vivís	viviste	vivisteis	vivías	vivíais
vive	viven	vivió	vivieron	vivía	vivían

VOLVER (TO COME BACK)

PRESENT		PRETERITE		IMPERFECT	
vuelvo	volvemos	volví	volvimos	volvía	volvíamos
vuelves	volvéis	volviste	volvisteis	volvías	volvíais
vuelve	vuelven	volvió	volvieron	volvía	volvían

ANSWER KEY

CHAPTER 1

1. h
2. c
3. g
4. i
5. a
6. d
7. b
8. e
9. j
10. f
11. b
12. b
13. c
14. a
15. c

CHAPTER 2

1. sensación
2. depresión
3. pesimismo
4. invención
5. celebración
6. curioso/a
7. urgente
8. prosperidad
9. experiencia
10. optimismo
11. geography
12. artist
13. pharmacy
14. nation
15. fabulous

16. paradise
17. humanity
18. dormitory
19. professor
20. museum

CHAPTER 3

1. Circle *Martín*, underline *está en la cocina*.
2. Circle *Anita*, underline *tiene zapatos negros*.
3. Circle *Yo*, underline *soy de los Estados Unidos*.
4. Circle *Los ojos de Antonieta*, underline *son azules*.
5. Circle *La computadora*, underline *es nueva*.
6. Circle *Miguel*, underline *tiene tres hermanos*.
7. Circle *Usted*, underline *es muy inteligente*.
8. Circle *Nosotros*, underline *vamos a la fiesta*.
9. Circle *El teatro*, underline *es bonito*.
10. Circle *Tu hermano*, underline *está en México*.
11. b
12. b
13. a
14. b
15. b

CHAPTER 4

1. la mano
2. la mesa
3. la piel
4. el personaje
5. el agua
6. la actriz
7. el niño
8. el rey
9. la hija

10. el/la artista
11. unas nueces
12. un águila
13. unos mapas
14. una pluma
15. unas fotos
16. el garaje
17. la decisión
18. los relojes
19. el barril
20. las motos

CHAPTER 5

1. saludar

Person	Singular	Plural
1st	yo saludo	nosotros saludamos nosotras saludamos
2nd	tú saludas	vosotros saludáis vosotras saludáis
3rd	él saluda ella saluda usted saluda	ellos saludan ellas saludan ustedes saludan

2. aprender

Person	Singular	Plural
1st	yo aprendo	nosotros aprendemos nosotras aprendemos
2nd	tú aprendes	vosotros aprendéis vosotras aprendéis
3rd	él aprende ella aprende usted aprende	ellos aprenden ellas aprenden ustedes aprenden

3. corre

4. viven
5. abro
6. estudiáis
7. comes
8. preparamos
9. lee
10. escriben
11. comprendo
12. regresáis

CHAPTER 6

1. b
2. c
3. a
4. d
5. e
6. f
7. pensar

Person	Singular	Plural
1st	yo pienso	nosotros pensamos nosotras pensamos
2nd	tú piensas	vosotros pensáis vosotras pensáis
3rd	él piensa ella piensa usted piensa	ellos piensan ellas piensan ustedes piensan

8. destruir

Person	Singular	Plural
1st	yo destruyo	nosotros destruimos nosotras destruimos
2nd	tú destruyes	vosotros destruís vosotras destruís

3rd	él destruye	ellos destruyen
	ella destruye	ellas destruyen
	usted destruye	ustedes destruyen

CHAPTER 7

1. tengo
2. eres
3. vais
4. van
5. conozco
6. somos
7. veo
8. Hay
9. tiene
10. vengo
11. b
12. c
13. a
14. b
15. c
16. b

CHAPTER 8

1. guapas
2. joven
3. buenos
4. vieja
5. feliz
6. Tengo un carro nuevo.
7. Ese perro es grande./Es grande ese perro.
8. Marta es hermosa./Es hermosa Marta.
9. Esas mochilas son vuestras./Son vuestras esas mochilas.
10. ¿Es tuyo aquel libro?/¿Aquel libro es tuyo?

CHAPTER 9

1. Soy
2. Es
3. Estáis
4. Eres
5. Son
6. es
7. Somos
8. Están
9. es
10. Estás
11. Mi jefe es rico.
12. Katie tiene nueve años.
13. Tomamos leche.
14. Los niños saben hablar alemán.
15. Hay dos manzanas en la refrigeradora.
16. ¿Tomas el autobús a la escuela?

CHAPTER 10

1. finalmente
2. nerviosamente
3. claramente
4. raramente
5. brevemente
6. algo
7. muy
8. Por supuesto
9. un poco
10. acá
11. luego
12. tanto
13. también
14. siempre

15. mucho

CHAPTER 11

1. Ninguno de mis amigos vive allí.
2. No necesitamos nada.
3. Nunca estudio con nadie.
4. ¿No queréis ir a la fiesta?
5. No hay nada en la refrigeradora.
6. Nunca coméis desayuno.
7. No conozco a nungún niño americano.
8. Nunca voy al gimnasio.
9. Los alumnos no tienen una computadora.
10. No amo a nadie.
11. tampoco
12. sino
13. también
14. pero
15. también
16. sino
17. pero
18. tampoco
19. también
20. sino

CHAPTER 12

1. Circle *sombrero*, underline *amigo*.
2. Circle *tarea*, underline *profesora*.
3. Circle *comida*, underline *perro*.
4. Circle *suéter*, underline *señora*.
5. Circle *sopa*, underline *niño*.
6. Francisco lo tiene.
7. ¿Lo veis?
8. La leemos.

9.   El muchacho lo escribe.
10. Yo la veo.
11. les
12. nos
13. me
14. le
15. te
16. Te los mando.
17. Se la presto.
18. Se la enseño.
19. Nos la compra.
20. ¿Me la traes?

CHAPTER 13

1.   más
2.   menos
3.   tanto como
4.   más
5.   mejor
6.   tanta
7.   menos
8.   menor
9.   peor
10. más
11. el más paciente
12. la menos diplomática
13. el/la menos inteligente
14. el/la mejor
15. la menor
16. el/la peor
17. el/la más fácil
18. el menos rápido
19. el menor
20. el menos caro

21. El pan es riquísimo.
22. La niña es traviesísima.
23. El profesor es malísimo.
24. La calles es larguísima.
25. Estoy felicísimo/a.

CHAPTER 14

1. El gato está debajo de la mesa.
2. El gato está dentro de la caja.
3. El gato está encima de la cama.
4. El gato está delante de la televisión.
5. El gato está lejos de la niña.
6. b
7. b
8. a
9. c
10. c
11. b
12. a
13. c

CHAPTER 15

1. Me baño todos los días.
2. Zoila se prueba los zapatos.
3. Mi padre se alza a las seis de la mañana.
4. La señora se quita los lentes.
5. ¿Te lavas la cara en la mañana?
6. Mi mejor amigo nunca se quita el sombrero.
7. Federico se duerme a las once.
8. La profesora se sienta sobre el escritorio.

9. cansarse

Person	Singular	Plural
1st	yo me canso	nosotros nos cansamos nosotras nos cansamos
2nd	tú te cansas	vosotros os cansáis vosotras os cansáis
3rd	él se cansa ella se cansa uted se cansa	ellos se cansan ellas se cansan ustedes se cansan

10. enojarse

Person	Singular	Plural
1st	yo me enojo	nosotros nos enojamos nosotras nos enojamos
2nd	tú te enojas	vosotros os enojáis vosotras os enojáis
3rd	él se enoja ella se enoja uted se enoja	ellos se enojan ellas se enojan ustedes se enojan

11. irse

Person	Singular	Plural
1st	yo me voy	nosotros nos vamos nosotras nos vamos
2nd	tú te vas	vosotros os vais vosotras os vais
3rd	él se va ella se va uted se va	ellos se van ellas se van ustedes se van

12. reírse

Person	Singular	Plural
1st	yo me río	nosotros nos reímos nosotras nos reímos
2nd	tú te ríes	vosotros os reís vosotras os reís
3rd	él se ríe ella se ríe uted se ríe	ellos se ríen ellas se ríen ustedes se ríen

CHAPTER 16

1. vendió
2. comí
3. corristeis
4. cerraste
5. vestió
6. oyeron
7. llegué
8. prefirió
9. rezó
10. dormimos
11. salieron
12. ganó
13. di
14. fuimos
15. visteis
16. condujiste
17. produjeron
18. estuvo
19. traje
20. fue

21. podisteis
22. tuviste
23. dijeron
24. supimos

CHAPTER 17

1. ibais
2. recibías
3. era
4. leían
5. veíais
6. corrían
7. iban
8. erais
9. tenías
10. llegábamos
11. veía
12. eran
13. aburría
14. esperaba
15. éramos
16. era
17. leíais
18. mandabas
19. bañaban
20. vivía/iba

CHAPTER 18

1. b
2. b.
3. a
4. b
5. a

6. b
7. se levantó
8. era/creí
9. dio
10. empezó
11. lloraba
12. entré/vi
13. era
14. comió
15. se olvidó
16. hacía